Contents

Fish Illustrations: Trevor Hawkins

Published in 2019 by
Australian Fishing Network Pty Ltd
PO Box 544, Croydon, VIC 3136
Tel: (03) 9729 8788
Fax: (03) 9729 7833
Email: sales@afn.com.au
Website: www.afn.com.au

ISBN 9781 8651 3369 0

DISCLAIMER

The tide times and heights in this book were derived from the program* WXTide32 *and are predictions. While they are as accurate as possible, they should be used as a guide only. Local conditions and changes can cause variations, so consult a website such as the* Bureau of Meteorology Oceanographic Services, (www.bom.gov.au/oceanography/tides) *as close as possible to the tide date and time before your fishing trip for the most up-to-date information and if you require certified information. The publisher, Australian Fishing Network, advises that the information in this guide should not be used for navigation and should not be relied on for crucial situations.

'Solunar' theory suggests all creatures great and small respond in some way to the influences of both the Sun and the Moon during the course of a day.

This book lists the peak activity times along with the moon phases and it should become an indispensable tool for when you're planning a trip.
The peak activity times are presented in this book to simulate the logical progression of the Moon as it orbits the Earth. The first is the minor peak at moonrise, no matter what time of day at which it occurs. The second is the major peak when the moon is directly overhead, the third is the minor peak at moonset and the fourth is the major peak when the moon is directly overhead on the opposite side of the globe.

Solunar (solar and lunar) theory is one of nature's mysteries which many of us find difficult to consider with any merit. A number of books, tables and articles have been written on the subject of lunar and solar influences on animal behaviour. Solunar theory suggests all creatures great and small respond in some way to the influences of both the Sun and the Moon during the course of a day. Specifically this response is often seen as an increase or decrease in activity level. Increased activity periods have often been referred to as peak or prime times.
The combination of centrifugal force produced by the Earth's rotation and the Moon's daily crossing of the sky generates our tides. Such enormous force is produced by these phenomena that it causes the Earth's surface to bulge up to 16 centimetres. Could lunar cycles impact on man? You be the judge. The human gestation period is 266 days, the average synodic interval between two consecutive new Moons is 29.530589 days; 266 divided by 29.530589 equals 9.008 lunar months. Sound familiar? Man is made up of approximately 80 per cent water. We know what happens tidally to huge bodies of water. Do you think there is a remote possibility that we too could unknowingly experience the effects of this heavenly sphere?

It is important to understand that what influences one creature may not influence another in any circumstance. For example there are a number of intertidal organisms that are most active when submerged by an incoming tide, creatures such as barnacles, green crabs, snails, clams, and oysters. Others, like soldier crabs and shorebirds, are especially adapted to feed on beaches exposed at low tide. The lower the creature's order in the animal kingdom the more likely it is to respond to solar and lunar stimuli.

LIGHT THEORY

The light theory suggests that light levels during the day and night dictate feeding activity times. For example it is said that fishing is better on the mornings immediately leading up to and following the period of new Moon because the fish have been unable to feed during the periods of low light during the night. Fishing is also said to be good during the nights leading up to and following the full Moon because of increased evening light levels.

SOLAR THEORY

To some extent the solar theory is reliant upon seasonal changes, therefore I have provided you with a brief summary of the seasonal patterns and how they influence the Southern Hemisphere.

The principle of the solar theory works on the various instances of the Sun's rise, upper transit, set, and lower transit to identify the peak activity periods. Following a long period of darkness the animal kingdom is given a kick-start to the day as dawn approaches. Many creatures stir from their rest period and warm with the Sun to commence the daily routine of food gathering. All animal life has a preferred temperature range and fish are no exception to this rule. It is said that seasonal conditions may dictate when particular fish species will commence to feed.

So although dawn and dusk have been historically noted as prime fishing times if we review the seasonal fluctuations in day and night time temperatures we may see cause for reassessing our reliance on these times. For example during the colder months peak feeding times may coincide during the warmest time of the day; just after midday when the water temperatures have increased to a more preferred level. Conversely, during the warmer months peak feeding times may align with the coolest times of the day; dusk 'til dawn.

SEASONS

Point A
Northern Hemisphere during fall. The Sun is high overhead at the equator and rays from the Sun fall equally on both the Southern and Northern Hemispheres.

Point B
Northern Hemisphere during winter. A lesser amount of the Sun's rays fall on the Northern Hemisphere where the Sun is low in the sky.

Point C
Northern Hemisphere during springtime. The Sun is high overhead at the equator and rays from the Sun fall equally on both the Southern and Northern Hemispheres.

Point D
Northern Hemisphere during summertime. A majority of the Sun's rays fall on the Northern Hemisphere where the Sun is high overhead.

A N Fall S
B N Winter S
C N Spring S
D N Summer S

LUNAR THEORY

To help you understand the lunar theory in more depth I have provided a brief outline of the various lunar phases. When you watch the Moon over a course of several days you will see that its appearance changes. The varying appearances called 'phases' depend upon the relative positions of the Sun and Moon.

MOON PHASES

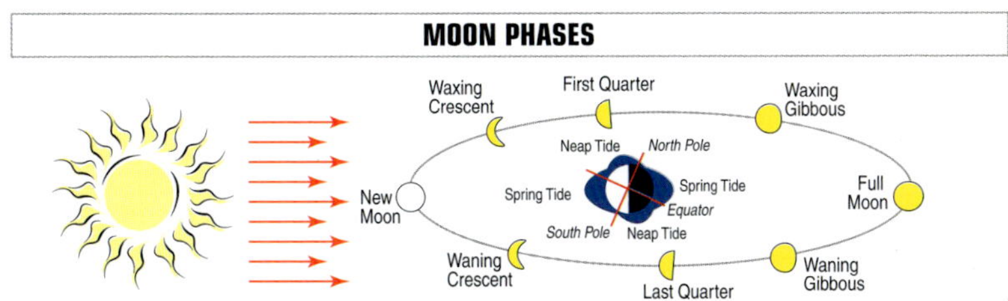

NEW MOON

When the Moon is between the Sun and the Earth we cannot see any of the illuminated side of the Moon, the Moon is dark, we call this phase the new Moon and it is the beginning of a new lunar month. The Moon rises and sets with the Sun during the new Moon. The gravitational forces exerted on the Earth by the Moon and the Sun is greatest at this time. The first of the spring tides for the lunar month occurs during this period.

FIRST QUARTER

The amount of lighted surface visible from the Earth begins to grow and we see a waxing crescent Moon. When the Moon reaches the first quarter we see half of it lit. The Moon rises during the middle of the day and is overhead about dusk and sets around midnight. The Moon's illuminated side will appear on the right in the Northern Hemisphere. The gravitational forces on the Earth have reduced since the new Moon and now the combined pull of the Moon and the Sun is at a minimum for the lunar month. The first of the neap tides for the Lunar month occurs at this time.

FULL MOON

As the illuminated portion grows we have a waxing gibbous Moon. The full Moon occurs when the Moon reaches the side of the Earth opposite from the Sun. It appears large and bright. The Moon rises as the Sun is setting—it is overhead about midnight and sets close to dawn. The gravitational forces on the Earth have increased since the first quarter and now the combined pull of the Moon and the Sun is at a maximum again for the lunar month, the second of the spring tides occur.

LAST QUARTER

The gravitational forces on the Earth have reduced since the full Moon and now the combined pull of the Moon and the Sun is at a minimum again for the lunar month. The second of the neap tides for the lunar month occurs at this time. As a waning crescent, the Moon diminishes to a thin sliver, returning to a new Moon after approximately 29.5 solar days or one lunar month. As the Moon revolves around the Earth it rotates on its own axis at the same rate it revolves, therefore the Moon always keeps the same face toward the Earth.

TIDAL FORCES

As the Earth rotates on its axis once every 24 hours relative to the Sun, and 24 hours and 53 minutes relative to the Moon; the Moon rises approximately 53 minutes later with respect to the Sun each day. This delay or lagging can be seen in the variation of tides from day to day.

The principle of the lunar theory works on the various instances of the Moon's rise, upper transit, set, and lower transit to identify the peak activity periods. This theory can also take into account the various lunar phases and the proximity (apogee and perigee) of the Moon to the Earth during the period of one lunation (new Moon to new Moon). Because the Moon orbits the Earth on an elliptical path, the distance between the two is always changing. The Moon has less gravitational influence on the Earth around the time of apogee when the distance between the two bodies is at a maximum. Greater gravitational influence occurs around the time of perigee when the distance between the Earth and the Moon is at a minimum.

SOLUNAR THEORY

Solunar theory accounts for the peaks associated with both the solar and lunar theories. It also incorporates the Sun's lower transit (midnight), and it also flags the coinciding times of peaks from the other theories. In other words it takes an each way bet on the three individual theories. Additionally the solunar theory recognises the gravitational effect on the Earth from the combined force produced by the Moon and the Sun in tandem. This gravitational force changes with the seasons, with the phases of the Moon, and with the Sun and Moon's proximity to Earth.

EFFECTS ON FISHING

Fishing wise, catch rates are often said to be higher around the new and full Moon phases. This makes sense when you consider the increased gravitational influence on the Earth during these periods. However this is further bolstered if you consider that during these times we are provided with three windows of peak activity level during general daylight hours, each coinciding with dawn, noon, or dusk. Around the period of new Moon, the Moon is in harmony with the Sun, they rise, transit and set together. During the period of full Moon, the Moon and Sun directly oppose each other, the Moon sets when the Sun rises, the Moon is underfoot at noon, and the Moon rises at Sun set. Whether or not the increased activity levels in lower organisms is the catalyst for larger and perhaps predatory creatures to begin feeding is arguable. Your observations will also show increased activity levels in the non predatory herbivore family during the peak times.

FEEDING PATTERNS

Does activity occur outside of these peak periods? Of course. Remember not all species will react in an identical manner during the peak times. The bottom line is fish don't always feel hungry! They follow certain feeding patterns but aren't totally immune to sampling the odd tid-bit throughout the course of the day. As with most creatures, strength is gained through struggle; and only the fittest and strongest survive in the wild. While minimum work for maximum return is the hallmark of big fish, a fish's condition and health must also be maintained through foraging for food. Natural rhythms aside, fish are also subject to local conditions such as the various fluctuations in air temperature, barometric pressure, water levels, water clarity, and water temperature. These should all be considered when using the tables.

BITE TIME ADJUSTMENTS (Minutes)

Approximate variation times only, taken from various sources.

Location	Minutes	Location	Minutes	Location	Minutes
Apollo Bay	+5	Halls Gap	+10	Port Albert	-5
Ballarat	+5	Hamilton	+10	Port Fairy	+10
Bemm River	-15	Hastings	0	Port Welshpool	-5
Bendigo	0	Horsham	+10	Portland	+10
Bendoc	-15	Inverloch	0	San Semo	0
Cann River	-15	Lakes Entrance	-10	Shallow Inlet	-5
Carrum	0	Mallacoota	-20	Swan Hill	+5
Dargo	-5	Marlo	-15	Tamboon	-15
Dartmouth	-10	McLoughlins Beach	-5	Torquay	0
Echuca	0	Melbourne	0	Walhalla	-5
Eildon	0	Mildura	+10	Wangaratta	-5
Geelong	0	Omeo	-10	Warnambool	+10
Golden Beach	-5	Ouyen	+10	Wilsons Promontory	-5

POPULAR TIDE ADJUSTMENTS

Location	Adjustment
Altona	+3hrs 25min
Anderson Inlet	+10min
Anglesea	-30min
Apollo Bay	-25min
Barwon Heads	+15min
Black Rock	+3hrs 2min
Cape Otway	-30min
Cape Patterson	0
Cape Schanack	0
Carrum	+3hrs 15min
Corinella	+1hr 8min
Cnr Inlet Ent.	+25min
Cowes	+1hr 15min
Dromana	+3hrs 20min
Flinders	+48min
Frankston	+3hrs 20min
Geelong	+3hrs 30min
Golden Beach	-1hr 30min
Gunnamatta	-25min
Hastings	+1hr 15min
Hovell Pile	+3hrs 20min
Inverloch	+20min
Kilcunda	+10min
K. Is (Franklin)	-40min
K. Is(Grassy)	-10min
K. Is(Surprise Bay)	-40min
Lake Tyers	-2hrs 57min
Lakes Entrance	-2hrs 50min
Lang Lang	+1hr 55min
Lochspot	-1hr 30min
Lorne	-20min
Mahers Landing	+1hr 30min
Mallacoota Inlet	-2hrs 38min
Maribynong Riv'	+3hrs 15min
McLoughins	+2hrs 25min
McLoughlins Bch	-1hr
Melbourne	+3hrs 30min
Mordialloc	+3hrs 5min
Mornington	+3hrs 20min
New Haven	+1hr 25min
No. 1 W Ch (Annulus)	+50min
No. 2 S Ch Light	+1hr 10min
No. 8 S Ch Light	+2hrs 30min
Point Cook	+3hrs 10min
Port Albert Pier	+1hr 30min
Port Fairy	-51min
Port Phillip Hds	0
Rabbit Island	+10min
Port Welshpool Pier	+1hr 21min
Portland	-50min
Portlarington	+3hrs 15min
Portsea	+1hr 20min
Queenscliff	+35min
Refuge Cove	+ 36min
Rhyll	+1hr
Rip Bank	-15min
Rosebud	+3hrs 20min
Rye	+3hrs
Sandringham	+3hrs 20min
Seal Rock	0
Seaspray	-3hrs 11min
Shallow Inlet	+13min
Singapore Deep	- 25min
Sorrento	+2hrs 15min
S. Ch Pile Light	+3hrs 10min
St Kilda	+3hrs 20min
St Leonards	+3hrs 15min
Stony Point	+1hr
Swan Island Dock	+2hrs
Tarwin River	+3hrs
Tooradin	+1hr 45min
Venus Bay	0
Warratah Bay	0
Warrnambool	-59min
Welshpool Pier	+1hr 30min
Werribee River	+3hrs 15min
W. Ch Pile Light	+3hrs 10min
Williamstown	+3hrs 25min
Woolami	0

Port Phillip Heads

Day	Date		Tide 1		
Sun	01		12:06 AM	(1.3)	**H**
Mon	02		1:10 AM	(1.4)	**H**
Tue	03		2:07 AM	(1.5)	**H**
Wed	04		2:59 AM	(1.6)	**H**
Thu	05		3:49 AM	(1.6)	**H**
Fri	06		4:38 AM	(1.6)	**H**
Sat	07		5:27 AM	(1.5)	**H**
Sun	08		6:16 AM	(1.4)	**H**
Mon	09		12:28 AM	(0.3)	L
Tue	10		1:18 AM	(0.3)	L
Wed	11		2:14 AM	(0.4)	L
Thu	12		3:18 AM	(0.4)	L
Fri	13		4:26 AM	(0.4)	L
Sat	14	○	5:29 AM	(0.4)	L
Sun	15		12:03 AM	(1.2)	**H**
Mon	16		12:54 AM	(1.3)	**H**
Tue	17		1:38 AM	(1.3)	**H**
Wed	18		2:18 AM	(1.4)	**H**
Thu	19		2:55 AM	(1.4)	**H**
Fri	20		3:32 AM	(1.4)	**H**
Sat	21		4:09 AM	(1.4)	**H**
Sun	22		4:48 AM	(1.4)	**H**
Mon	23		5:30 AM	(1.4)	**H**
Tue	24		6:19 AM	(1.3)	**H**
Wed	25		12:26 AM	(0.3)	L
Thu	26		1:30 AM	(0.3)	L
Fri	27		2:45 AM	(0.4)	L
Sat	28		4:07 AM	(0.4)	L
Sun	29	●	5:24 AM	(0.4)	L
Mon	30		12:06 AM	(1.4)	**H**

During Daylight Savings Time add one hour to the times stated below.

SEPTEMBER 2019

Tide 2		Tide 3		Tide 4	
6:37 AM	(0.2) L	1:06 PM	(1.4) **H**	7:13 PM	(0.4) L
7:32 AM	(0.2) L	1:51 PM	(1.5) **H**	8:01 PM	(0.3) L
8:22 AM	(0.2) L	2:33 PM	(1.5) **H**	8:46 PM	(0.2) L
9:09 AM	(0.3) L	3:14 PM	(1.5) **H**	9:30 PM	(0.2) L
9:53 AM	(0.3) L	3:53 PM	(1.5) **H**	10:14 PM	(0.1) L
10:37 AM	(0.4) L	4:32 PM	(1.5) **H**	10:57 PM	(0.2) L
11:20 AM	(0.5) L	5:12 PM	(1.4) **H**	11:41 PM	(0.2) L
12:05 PM	(0.6) L	5:53 PM	(1.4) **H**		
7:09 AM	(1.3) **H**	12:53 PM	(0.7) L	6:39 PM	(1.3) **H**
8:07 AM	(1.3) **H**	1:50 PM	(0.8) L	7:33 PM	(1.2) **H**
9:10 AM	(1.2) **H**	3:00 PM	(0.8) L	8:37 PM	(1.1) **H**
10:17 AM	(1.2) **H**	4:18 PM	(0.7) L	9:50 PM	(1.1) **H**
11:16 AM	(1.2) **H**	5:28 PM	(0.7) L	11:02 PM	(1.1) **H**
12:05 PM	(1.3) **H**	6:19 PM	(0.6) L		
6:22 AM	(0.4) L	12:46 PM	(1.3) **H**	7:00 PM	(0.5) L
7:07 AM	(0.4) L	1:22 PM	(1.4) **H**	7:36 PM	(0.4) L
7:47 AM	(0.4) L	1:55 PM	(1.4) **H**	8:09 PM	(0.3) L
8:24 AM	(0.4) L	2:26 PM	(1.4) **H**	8:41 PM	(0.3) L
8:59 AM	(0.4) L	2:55 PM	(1.4) **H**	9:12 PM	(0.2) L
9:33 AM	(0.4) L	3:23 PM	(1.4) **H**	9:43 PM	(0.2) L
10:06 AM	(0.5) L	3:50 PM	(1.4) **H**	10:16 PM	(0.2) L
10:40 AM	(0.6) L	4:20 PM	(1.3) **H**	10:52 PM	(0.2) L
11:18 AM	(0.6) L	4:55 PM	(1.3) **H**	11:35 PM	(0.2) L
12:03 PM	(0.7) L	5:41 PM	(1.3) **H**		
7:16 AM	(1.2) **H**	1:00 PM	(0.7) L	6:43 PM	(1.2) **H**
8:23 AM	(1.2) **H**	2:12 PM	(0.7) L	8:03 PM	(1.2) **H**
9:35 AM	(1.2) **H**	3:33 PM	(0.7) L	9:31 PM	(1.2) **H**
10:44 AM	(1.2) **H**	4:51 PM	(0.5) L	10:54 PM	(1.3) **H**
11:45 AM	(1.3) **H**	5:56 PM	(0.4) L		
6:28 AM	(0.3) L	12:37 PM	(1.4) **H**	6:50 PM	(0.3) L

POPULAR TIDE ADJUSTMENTS

Location	Adjustment
Altona	+3hrs 25min
Anderson Inlet	+10min
Anglesea	-30min
Apollo Bay	-25min
Barwon Heads	+15min
Black Rock	+3hrs 2min
Cape Otway	-30min
Cape Patterson	0
Cape Schanack	0
Carrum	+3hrs 15min
Corinella	+1hr 8min
Cnr Inlet Ent.	+25min
Cowes	+1hr 15min
Dromana	+3hrs 20min
Flinders	+48min
Frankston	+3hrs 20min
Geelong	+3hrs 30min
Golden Beach	-1hr 30min
Gunnamatta	-25min
Hastings	+1hr 15min
Hovell Pile	+3hrs 20min
Inverloch	+20min
Kilcunda	+10min
K. Is (Franklin)	-40min
K. Is(Grassy)	-10min
K. Is(Surprise Bay)	-40min
Lake Tyers	-2hrs 57min
Lakes Entrance	-2hrs 50min
Lang Lang	+1hr 55min
Lochspot	-1hr 30min
Lorne	-20min
Mahers Landing	+1hr 30min
Mallacoota Inlet	-2hrs 38min
Maribynong Riv'	+3hrs 15min
McLoughins	+2hrs 25min
McLoughlins Bch	-1hr
Melbourne	+3hrs 30min
Mordialloc	+3hrs 5min
Mornington	+3hrs 20min
New Haven	+1hr 25min
No. 1 W Ch (Annulus)	+50min
No. 2 S Ch Light	+1hr 10min
No. 8 S Ch Light	+2hrs 30min
Point Cook	+3hrs 10min
Port Albert Pier	+1hr 30min
Port Fairy	-51min
Port Phillip Hds	0
Rabbit Island	+10min
Port Welshpool Pier	+1hr 21min
Portland	-50min
Portlarington	+3hrs 15min
Portsea	+1hr 20min
Queenscliff	+35min
Refuge Cove	+ 36min
Rhyll	+1hr
Rip Bank	-15min
Rosebud	+3hrs 20min
Rye	+3hrs
Sandringham	+3hrs 20min
Seal Rock	0
Seaspray	-3hrs 11min
Shallow Inlet	+13min
Singapore Deep	- 25min
Sorrento	+2hrs 15min
S. Ch Pile Light	+3hrs 10min
St Kilda	+3hrs 20min
St Leonards	+3hrs 15min
Stony Point	+1hr
Swan Island Dock	+2hrs
Tarwin River	+3hrs
Tooradin	+1hr 45min
Venus Bay	0
Warratah Bay	0
Warrnambool	-59min
Welshpool Pier	+1hr 30min
Werribee River	+3hrs 15min
W. Ch Pile Light	+3hrs 10min
Williamstown	+3hrs 25min
Woolami	0

Port Phillip Heads

Day	Date		Tide 1
Tue	01		1:07 AM (1.5) **H**
Wed	02		2:00 AM (1.6) **H**
Thu	03		2:48 AM (1.6) **H**
Fri	04		3:35 AM (1.6) **H**
Sat	05		4:19 AM (1.6) **H**
Sun	06		5:03 AM (1.5) **H**
Mon	07		5:47 AM (1.4) **H**
Tue	08		6:32 AM (1.3) **H**
Wed	09		12:38 AM (0.4) L
Thu	10		1:31 AM (0.5) L
Fri	11		2:34 AM (0.5) L
Sat	12		3:46 AM (0.6) L
Sun	13		4:56 AM (0.5) L
Mon	14	○	5:55 AM (0.5) L
Tue	15		12:35 AM (1.3) **H**
Wed	16		1:17 AM (1.4) **H**
Thu	17		1:56 AM (1.5) **H**
Fri	18		2:33 AM (1.5) **H**
Sat	19		3:10 AM (1.5) **H**
Sun	20		3:46 AM (1.5) **H**
Mon	21		4:24 AM (1.5) **H**
Tue	22		5:05 AM (1.4) **H**
Wed	23		5:52 AM (1.4) **H**
Thu	24		12:02 AM (0.3) L
Fri	25		1:07 AM (0.4) L
Sat	26		2:25 AM (0.5) L
Sun	27		3:50 AM (0.5) L
Mon	28	●	5:09 AM (0.5) L
Tue	29		12:02 AM (1.5) **H**
Wed	30		12:59 AM (1.6) **H**
Thu	31		1:49 AM (1.7) **H**

During Daylight Savings Time add one hour to the times stated below.

OCTOBER 2019

Tide 2		Tide 3		Tide 4	
7:22 AM	(0.3) L	1:23 PM	(1.5) **H**	7:38 PM	(0.2) L
8:11 AM	(0.3) L	2:06 PM	(1.5) **H**	8:23 PM	(0.1) L
8:55 AM	(0.3) L	2:47 PM	(1.5) **H**	9:06 PM	(0.1) L
9:38 AM	(0.4) L	3:26 PM	(1.5) **H**	9:47 PM	(0.1) L
10:19 AM	(0.5) L	4:05 PM	(1.5) **H**	10:28 PM	(0.1) L
11:00 AM	(0.5) L	4:44 PM	(1.4) **H**	11:09 PM	(0.2) L
11:42 AM	(0.6) L	5:24 PM	(1.3) **H**	11:52 PM	(0.3) L
12:27 PM	(0.7) L	6:10 PM	(1.2) **H**		
7:22 AM	(1.3) **H**	1:20 PM	(0.7) L	7:05 PM	(1.1) **H**
8:18 AM	(1.2) **H**	2:24 PM	(0.7) L	8:13 PM	(1.1) **H**
9:19 AM	(1.2) **H**	3:36 PM	(0.7) L	9:30 PM	(1.1) **H**
10:19 AM	(1.2) **H**	4:44 PM	(0.6) L	10:44 PM	(1.1) **H**
11:13 AM	(1.2) **H**	5:36 PM	(0.5) L	11:45 PM	(1.2) **H**
11:58 AM	(1.2) **H**	6:19 PM	(0.4) L		
6:43 AM	(0.5) L	12:37 PM	(1.3) **H**	6:56 PM	(0.3) L
7:24 AM	(0.5) L	1:13 PM	(1.3) **H**	7:30 PM	(0.3) L
8:02 AM	(0.5) L	1:45 PM	(1.3) **H**	8:03 PM	(0.2) L
8:38 AM	(0.5) L	2:16 PM	(1.3) **H**	8:36 PM	(0.2) L
9:13 AM	(0.5) L	2:47 PM	(1.3) **H**	9:10 PM	(0.1) L
9:47 AM	(0.5) L	3:18 PM	(1.3) **H**	9:45 PM	(0.1) L
10:22 AM	(0.6) L	3:54 PM	(1.3) **H**	10:24 PM	(0.2) L
11:01 AM	(0.6) L	4:35 PM	(1.3) **H**	11:08 PM	(0.2) L
11:48 AM	(0.6) L	5:28 PM	(1.2) **H**		
6:46 AM	(1.3) **H**	12:46 PM	(0.6) L	6:38 PM	(1.2) **H**
7:48 AM	(1.2) **H**	1:55 PM	(0.6) L	8:03 PM	(1.2) **H**
8:57 AM	(1.2) **H**	3:12 PM	(0.5) L	9:32 PM	(1.2) **H**
10:05 AM	(1.2) **H**	4:26 PM	(0.4) L	10:53 PM	(1.3) **H**
11:08 AM	(1.3) **H**	5:30 PM	(0.3) L		
6:14 AM	(0.5) L	12:03 PM	(1.4) **H**	6:25 PM	(0.2) L
7:09 AM	(0.4) L	12:52 PM	(1.4) **H**	7:14 PM	(0.1) L
7:56 AM	(0.4) L	1:37 PM	(1.5) **H**	7:59 PM	(0.1) L

POPULAR TIDE ADJUSTMENTS

Location	Adjustment
Altona	+3hrs 25min
Anderson Inlet	+10min
Anglesea	-30min
Apollo Bay	-25min
Barwon Heads	+15min
Black Rock	+3hrs 2min
Cape Otway	-30min
Cape Patterson	0
Cape Schanack	0
Carrum	+3hrs 15min
Corinella	+1hr 8min
Cnr Inlet Ent.	+25min
Cowes	+1hr 15min
Dromana	+3hrs 20min
Flinders	+48min
Frankston	+3hrs 20min
Geelong	+3hrs 30min
Golden Beach	-1hr 30min
Gunnamatta	-25min
Hastings	+1hr 15min
Hovell Pile	+3hrs 20min
Inverloch	+20min
Kilcunda	+10min
K. Is (Franklin)	-40min
K. Is(Grassy)	-10min
K. Is(Surprise Bay)	-40min
Lake Tyers	-2hrs 57min
Lakes Entrance	-2hrs 50min
Lang Lang	+1hr 55min
Lochspot	-1hr 30min
Lorne	-20min
Mahers Landing	+1hr 30min
Mallacoota Inlet	-2hrs 38min
Maribynong Riv'	+3hrs 15min
McLoughins	+2hrs 25min
McLoughlins Bch	-1hr
Melbourne	+3hrs 30min
Mordialloc	+3hrs 5min
Mornington	+3hrs 20min
New Haven	+1hr 25min
No. 1 W Ch (Annulus)	+50min
No. 2 S Ch Light	+1hr 10min
No. 8 S Ch Light	+2hrs 30min
Point Cook	+3hrs 10min
Port Albert Pier	+1hr 30min
Port Fairy	-51min
Port Phillip Hds	0
Rabbit Island	+10min
Port Welshpool Pier	+1hr 21min
Portland	-50min
Portlarington	+3hrs 15min
Portsea	+1hr 20min
Queenscliff	+35min
Refuge Cove	+ 36min
Rhyll	+1hr
Rip Bank	-15min
Rosebud	+3hrs 20min
Rye	+3hrs
Sandringham	+3hrs 20min
Seal Rock	0
Seaspray	-3hrs 11min
Shallow Inlet	+13min
Singapore Deep	- 25min
Sorrento	+2hrs 15min
S. Ch Pile Light	+3hrs 10min
St Kilda	+3hrs 20min
St Leonards	+3hrs 15min
Stony Point	+1hr
Swan Island Dock	+2hrs
Tarwin River	+3hrs
Tooradin	+1hr 45min
Venus Bay	0
Warratah Bay	0
Warrnambool	-59min
Welshpool Pier	+1hr 30min
Werribee River	+3hrs 15min
W. Ch Pile Light	+3hrs 10min
Williamstown	+3hrs 25min
Woolami	0

Port Phillip Heads

Day	Date		Tide 1
Fri	01		2:35 AM (1.7) **H**
Sat	02		3:18 AM (1.7) **H**
Sun	03		3:59 AM (1.6) **H**
Mon	04		4:39 AM (1.6) **H**
Tue	05		5:17 AM (1.5) **H**
Wed	06		5:57 AM (1.4) **H**
Thu	07		6:38 AM (1.3) **H**
Fri	08		12:46 AM (0.5) L
Sat	09		1:45 AM (0.6) L
Sun	10		2:54 AM (0.7) L
Mon	11		4:09 AM (0.7) L
Tue	12	○	5:18 AM (0.6) L
Wed	13		12:10 AM (1.3) **H**
Thu	14		12:54 AM (1.4) **H**
Fri	15		1:35 AM (1.5) **H**
Sat	16		2:13 AM (1.5) **H**
Sun	17		2:50 AM (1.6) **H**
Mon	18		3:28 AM (1.6) **H**
Tue	19		4:06 AM (1.5) **H**
Wed	20		4:47 AM (1.5) **H**
Thu	21		5:31 AM (1.4) **H**
Fri	22		6:20 AM (1.3) **H**
Sat	23		12:50 AM (0.5) L
Sun	24		2:04 AM (0.6) L
Mon	25		3:26 AM (0.6) L
Tue	26		4:46 AM (0.6) L
Wed	27	●	5:55 AM (0.6) L
Thu	28		12:46 AM (1.6) **H**
Fri	29		1:35 AM (1.6) **H**
Sat	30		2:20 AM (1.7) **H**

During Daylight Savings Time add one hour to the times stated below.

NOVEMBER 2019

Tide 2		Tide 3		Tide 4	
8:40 AM	(0.4) L	2:20 PM	(1.5) **H**	8:41 PM	(0.0) L
9:22 AM	(0.5) L	3:01 PM	(1.4) **H**	9:22 PM	(0.1) L
10:02 AM	(0.5) L	3:40 PM	(1.4) **H**	10:01 PM	(0.2) L
10:42 AM	(0.5) L	4:20 PM	(1.3) **H**	10:39 PM	(0.2) L
11:22 AM	(0.6) L	5:01 PM	(1.2) **H**	11:18 PM	(0.3) L
12:05 PM	(0.6) L	5:47 PM	(1.2) **H**	11:59 PM	(0.4) L
12:52 PM	(0.6) L	6:42 PM	(1.1) **H**		
7:25 AM	(1.2) **H**	1:47 PM	(0.6) L	7:48 PM	(1.1) **H**
8:17 AM	(1.2) **H**	2:47 PM	(0.6) L	9:03 PM	(1.1) **H**
9:13 AM	(1.2) **H**	3:49 PM	(0.5) L	10:16 PM	(1.1) **H**
10:09 AM	(1.2) **H**	4:44 PM	(0.5) L	11:19 PM	(1.2) **H**
11:00 AM	(1.2) **H**	5:31 PM	(0.4) L		
6:13 AM	(0.6) L	11:45 AM	(1.2) **H**	6:13 PM	(0.3) L
6:59 AM	(0.6) L	12:26 PM	(1.3) **H**	6:52 PM	(0.2) L
7:40 AM	(0.6) L	1:04 PM	(1.3) **H**	7:29 PM	(0.1) L
8:18 AM	(0.5) L	1:41 PM	(1.3) **H**	8:06 PM	(0.1) L
8:54 AM	(0.5) L	2:18 PM	(1.3) **H**	8:44 PM	(0.1) L
9:31 AM	(0.5) L	2:57 PM	(1.3) **H**	9:23 PM	(0.1) L
10:09 AM	(0.5) L	3:40 PM	(1.3) **H**	10:06 PM	(0.2) L
10:51 AM	(0.5) L	4:29 PM	(1.3) **H**	10:53 PM	(0.2) L
11:39 AM	(0.5) L	5:29 PM	(1.2) **H**	11:47 PM	(0.3) L
12:35 PM	(0.5) L	6:41 PM	(1.2) **H**		
7:17 AM	(1.3) **H**	1:39 PM	(0.5) L	8:01 PM	(1.2) **H**
8:19 AM	(1.3) **H**	2:48 PM	(0.4) L	9:24 PM	(1.3) **H**
9:24 AM	(1.3) **H**	3:57 PM	(0.3) L	10:43 PM	(1.4) **H**
10:27 AM	(1.3) **H**	5:02 PM	(0.2) L	11:50 PM	(1.5) **H**
11:26 AM	(1.3) **H**	5:59 PM	(0.1) L		
6:52 AM	(0.6) L	12:20 PM	(1.4) **H**	6:50 PM	(0.1) L
7:41 AM	(0.5) L	1:10 PM	(1.4) **H**	7:36 PM	(0.1) L
8:25 AM	(0.5) L	1:56 PM	(1.4) **H**	8:19 PM	(0.1) L

POPULAR TIDE ADJUSTMENTS

Location	Adjustment
Altona	+3hrs 25min
Anderson Inlet	+10min
Anglesea	-30min
Apollo Bay	-25min
Barwon Heads	+15min
Black Rock	+3hrs 2min
Cape Otway	-30min
Cape Patterson	0
Cape Schanack	0
Carrum	+3hrs 15min
Corinella	+1hr 8min
Cnr Inlet Ent.	+25min
Cowes	+1hr 15min
Dromana	+3hrs 20min
Flinders	+48min
Frankston	+3hrs 20min
Geelong	+3hrs 30min
Golden Beach	-1hr 30min
Gunnamatta	-25min
Hastings	+1hr 15min
Hovell Pile	+3hrs 20min
Inverloch	+20min
Kilcunda	+10min
K. Is (Franklin)	-40min
K. Is(Grassy)	-10min
K. Is(Surprise Bay)	-40min
Lake Tyers	-2hrs 57min
Lakes Entrance	-2hrs 50min
Lang Lang	+1hr 55min
Lochspot	-1hr 30min
Lorne	-20min
Mahers Landing	+1hr 30min
Mallacoota Inlet	-2hrs 38min
Maribynong Riv'	+3hrs 15min
McLoughins	+2hrs 25min
McLoughlins Bch	-1hr
Melbourne	+3hrs 30min
Mordialloc	+3hrs 5min
Mornington	+3hrs 20min
New Haven	+1hr 25min
No. 1 W Ch (Annulus)	+50min
No. 2 S Ch Light	+1hr 10min
No. 8 S Ch Light	+2hrs 30min
Point Cook	+3hrs 10min
Port Albert Pier	+1hr 30min
Port Fairy	-51min
Port Phillip Hds	0
Rabbit Island	+10min
Port Welshpool Pier	+1hr 21min
Portland	-50min
Portlarington	+3hrs 15min
Portsea	+1hr 20min
Queenscliff	+35min
Refuge Cove	+ 36min
Rhyll	+1hr
Rip Bank	-15min
Rosebud	+3hrs 20min
Rye	+3hrs
Sandringham	+3hrs 20min
Seal Rock	0
Seaspray	-3hrs 11min
Shallow Inlet	+13min
Singapore Deep	- 25min
Sorrento	+2hrs 15min
S. Ch Pile Light	+3hrs 10min
St Kilda	+3hrs 20min
St Leonards	+3hrs 15min
Stony Point	+1hr
Swan Island Dock	+2hrs
Tarwin River	+3hrs
Tooradin	+1hr 45min
Venus Bay	0
Warratah Bay	0
Warrnambool	-59min
Welshpool Pier	+1hr 30min
Werribee River	+3hrs 15min
W. Ch Pile Light	+3hrs 10min
Williamstown	+3hrs 25min
Woolami	0

Port Phillip Heads

Day	Date		Tide 1
Sun	01		3:01 AM (1.7) **H**
Mon	02		3:39 AM (1.6) **H**
Tue	03		4:15 AM (1.6) **H**
Wed	04		4:50 AM (1.5) **H**
Thu	05		5:24 AM (1.4) **H**
Fri	06		5:59 AM (1.3) **H**
Sat	07		12:08 AM (0.5) L
Sun	08		12:58 AM (0.6) L
Mon	09		2:00 AM (0.7) L
Tue	10		3:11 AM (0.7) L
Wed	11		4:26 AM (0.8) L
Thu	12	○	5:34 AM (0.7) L
Fri	13		12:29 AM (1.4) **H**
Sat	14		1:13 AM (1.5) **H**
Sun	15		1:54 AM (1.5) **H**
Mon	16		2:33 AM (1.5) **H**
Tue	17		3:12 AM (1.6) **H**
Wed	18		3:51 AM (1.5) **H**
Thu	19		4:31 AM (1.5) **H**
Fri	20		5:12 AM (1.5) **H**
Sat	21		5:57 AM (1.4) **H**
Sun	22		12:34 AM (0.5) L
Mon	23		1:40 AM (0.6) L
Tue	24		2:54 AM (0.7) L
Wed	25		4:14 AM (0.7) L
Thu	26	●	5:31 AM (0.7) L
Fri	27		12:30 AM (1.5) **H**
Sat	28		1:20 AM (1.6) **H**
Sun	29		2:03 AM (1.6) **H**
Mon	30		2:42 AM (1.6) **H**
Tue	31		3:18 AM (1.6) **H**

During Daylight Savings Time add one hour to the times stated below.

DECEMBER 2019

Tide 2		Tide 3		Tide 4	
9:07 AM	(0.5) L	2:39 PM	(1.4) **H**	8:59 PM	(0.1) L
9:47 AM	(0.5) L	3:21 PM	(1.3) **H**	9:37 PM	(0.2) L
10:25 AM	(0.5) L	4:02 PM	(1.3) **H**	10:14 PM	(0.3) L
11:03 AM	(0.5) L	4:44 PM	(1.2) **H**	10:49 PM	(0.4) L
11:42 AM	(0.5) L	5:29 PM	(1.1) **H**	11:27 PM	(0.4) L
12:23 PM	(0.5) L	6:19 PM	(1.1) **H**		
6:37 AM	(1.3) **H**	1:08 PM	(0.5) L	7:18 PM	(1.1) **H**
7:20 AM	(1.2) **H**	1:58 PM	(0.5) L	8:25 PM	(1.1) **H**
8:08 AM	(1.2) **H**	2:51 PM	(0.5) L	9:34 PM	(1.1) **H**
9:01 AM	(1.2) **H**	3:46 PM	(0.4) L	10:41 PM	(1.2) **H**
9:56 AM	(1.2) **H**	4:39 PM	(0.3) L	11:39 PM	(1.3) **H**
10:49 AM	(1.2) **H**	5:29 PM	(0.3) L		
6:30 AM	(0.7) L	11:39 AM	(1.2) **H**	6:16 PM	(0.2) L
7:17 AM	(0.6) L	12:27 PM	(1.2) **H**	7:00 PM	(0.1) L
7:59 AM	(0.6) L	1:13 PM	(1.3) **H**	7:44 PM	(0.1) L
8:38 AM	(0.5) L	1:59 PM	(1.3) **H**	8:27 PM	(0.1) L
9:18 AM	(0.5) L	2:47 PM	(1.3) **H**	9:11 PM	(0.1) L
9:58 AM	(0.4) L	3:37 PM	(1.3) **H**	9:56 PM	(0.2) L
10:42 AM	(0.4) L	4:32 PM	(1.3) **H**	10:44 PM	(0.2) L
11:29 AM	(0.4) L	5:32 PM	(1.3) **H**	11:36 PM	(0.4) L
12:21 PM	(0.3) L	6:38 PM	(1.3) **H**		
6:47 AM	(1.4) **H**	1:18 PM	(0.3) L	7:50 PM	(1.3) **H**
7:42 AM	(1.3) **H**	2:20 PM	(0.3) L	9:07 PM	(1.3) **H**
8:42 AM	(1.3) **H**	3:26 PM	(0.2) L	10:24 PM	(1.4) **H**
9:46 AM	(1.3) **H**	4:32 PM	(0.2) L	11:33 PM	(1.4) **H**
10:49 AM	(1.3) **H**	5:32 PM	(0.2) L		
6:33 AM	(0.7) L	11:50 AM	(1.3) **H**	6:27 PM	(0.1) L
7:25 AM	(0.6) L	12:45 PM	(1.3) **H**	7:16 PM	(0.1) L
8:10 AM	(0.5) L	1:36 PM	(1.3) **H**	7:59 PM	(0.1) L
8:51 AM	(0.5) L	2:22 PM	(1.3) **H**	8:40 PM	(0.1) L
9:30 AM	(0.4) L	3:06 PM	(1.3) **H**	9:17 PM	(0.2) L

Port Phillip Heads

Day	Date	Tide 1
Wed	1	3:54 AM (1.5) **H**
Thu	2	4:26 AM (1.5) **H**
Fri	3	4:56 AM (1.4) **H**
Sat	4	5:26 AM (1.4) **H**
Sun	5	5:57 AM (1.3) **H**
Mon	6	12:24 AM (0.6) L
Tue	7	1:15 AM (0.7) L
Wed	8	2:18 AM (0.8) L
Thu	9	3:31 AM (0.8) L
Fri	10	4:48 AM (0.8) L
Sat	11 ○	12:02 AM (1.3) **H**
Sun	12	12:52 AM (1.4) **H**
Mon	13	1:36 AM (1.5) **H**
Tue	14	2:17 AM (1.5) **H**
Wed	15	2:56 AM (1.5) **H**
Thu	16	3:35 AM (1.5) **H**
Fri	17	4:13 AM (1.5) **H**
Sat	18	4:52 AM (1.5) **H**
Sun	19	5:33 AM (1.4) **H**
Mon	20	12:15 AM (0.5) L
Tue	21	1:12 AM (0.6) L
Wed	22	2:17 AM (0.7) L
Thu	23	3:34 AM (0.8) L
Fri	24	5:00 AM (0.8) L
Sat	25 ●	12:12 AM (1.4) **H**
Sun	26	1:03 AM (1.4) **H**
Mon	27	1:45 AM (1.5) **H**
Tue	28	2:22 AM (1.5) **H**
Wed	29	2:56 AM (1.5) **H**
Thu	30	3:28 AM (1.5) **H**
Fri	31	3:57 AM (1.4) **H**

POPULAR TIDE ADJUSTMENTS

Location	Adjustment
Altona	+3hrs 25min
Anderson Inlet	+10min
Anglesea	-30min
Apollo Bay	-25min
Barwon Heads	+15min
Black Rock	+3hrs 2min
Cape Otway	-30min
Cape Patterson	0
Cape Schanack	0
Carrum	+3hrs 15min
Corinella	+1hr 8min
Cnr Inlet Ent.	+25min
Cowes	+1hr 15min
Dromana	+3hrs 20min
Flinders	+48min
Frankston	+3hrs 20min
Geelong	+3hrs 30min
Golden Beach	-1hr 30min
Gunnamatta	-25min
Hastings	+1hr 15min
Hovell Pile	+3hrs 20min
Inverloch	+20min
Kilcunda	+10min
K. Is (Franklin)	-40min
K. Is(Grassy)	-10min
K. Is(Surprise Bay)	-40min
Lake Tyers	-2hrs 57min
Lakes Entrance	-2hrs 50min
Lang Lang	+1hr 55min
Lochspot	-1hr 30min
Lorne	-20min
Mahers Landing	+1hr 30min
Mallacoota Inlet	-2hrs 38min
Maribynong Riv'	+3hrs 15min
McLoughins	+2hrs 25min
McLoughlins Bch	-1hr
Melbourne	+3hrs 30min
Mordialloc	+3hrs 5min
Mornington	+3hrs 20min
New Haven	+1hr 25min
No. 1 W Ch (Annulus)	+50min
No. 2 S Ch Light	+1hr 10min
No. 8 S Ch Light	+2hrs 30min
Point Cook	+3hrs 10min
Port Albert Pier	+1hr 30min
Port Fairy	-51min
Port Phillip Hds	0
Rabbit Island	+10min
Port Welshpool Pier	+1hr 21min
Portland	-50min
Portlarington	+3hrs 15min
Portsea	+1hr 20min
Queenscliff	+35min
Refuge Cove	+ 36min
Rhyll	+1hr
Rip Bank	-15min
Rosebud	+3hrs 20min
Rye	+3hrs
Sandringham	+3hrs 20min
Seal Rock	0
Seaspray	-3hrs 11min
Shallow Inlet	+13min
Singapore Deep	- 25min
Sorrento	+2hrs 15min
S. Ch Pile Light	+3hrs 10min
St Kilda	+3hrs 20min
St Leonards	+3hrs 15min
Stony Point	+1hr
Swan Island Dock	+2hrs
Tarwin River	+3hrs
Tooradin	+1hr 45min
Venus Bay	0
Warratah Bay	0
Warrnambool	-59min
Welshpool Pier	+1hr 30min
Werribee River	+3hrs 15min
W. Ch Pile Light	+3hrs 10min
Williamstown	+3hrs 25min
Woolami	0

JANUARY 2020

Tide 2		Tide 3		Tide 4	
10:08 AM	(0.4) L	3:48 PM	(1.2) **H**	9:53 PM	(0.3) L
10:43 AM	(0.4) L	4:30 PM	(1.2) **H**	10:28 PM	(0.3) L
11:18 AM	(0.4) L	5:13 PM	(1.2) **H**	11:03 PM	(0.4) L
11:54 AM	(0.4) L	5:58 PM	(1.1) **H**	11:41 PM	(0.5) L
12:31 PM	(0.4) L	6:49 PM	(1.1) **H**		
6:31 AM	(1.3) **H**	1:13 PM	(0.4) L	7:47 PM	(1.1) **H**
7:11 AM	(1.2) **H**	2:00 PM	(0.4) L	8:51 PM	(1.1) **H**
7:59 AM	(1.2) **H**	2:53 PM	(0.3) L	9:59 PM	(1.2) **H**
8:54 AM	(1.1) **H**	3:50 PM	(0.3) L	11:05 PM	(1.3) **H**
9:55 AM	(1.1) **H**	4:48 PM	(0.2) L		
5:58 AM	(0.8) L	10:57 AM	(1.1) **H**	5:45 PM	(0.2) L
6:53 AM	(0.7) L	11:58 AM	(1.2) **H**	6:38 PM	(0.1) L
7:39 AM	(0.6) L	12:55 PM	(1.2) **H**	7:29 PM	(0.1) L
8:22 AM	(0.5) L	1:51 PM	(1.3) **H**	8:17 PM	(0.1) L
9:03 AM	(0.4) L	2:44 PM	(1.3) **H**	9:04 PM	(0.1) L
9:45 AM	(0.3) L	3:38 PM	(1.4) **H**	9:50 PM	(0.2) L
10:28 AM	(0.3) L	4:31 PM	(1.4) **H**	10:36 PM	(0.3) L
11:12 AM	(0.2) L	5:27 PM	(1.4) **H**	11:24 PM	(0.4) L
12:00 PM	(0.2) L	6:26 PM	(1.3) **H**		
6:16 AM	(1.4) **H**	12:52 PM	(0.2) L	7:30 PM	(1.3) **H**
7:04 AM	(1.3) **H**	1:48 PM	(0.2) L	8:40 PM	(1.3) **H**
7:59 AM	(1.3) **H**	2:50 PM	(0.2) L	9:55 PM	(1.3) **H**
9:01 AM	(1.2) **H**	3:56 PM	(0.2) L	11:09 PM	(1.3) **H**
10:09 AM	(1.2) **H**	5:03 PM	(0.2) L		
6:14 AM	(0.7) L	11:20 AM	(1.2) **H**	6:04 PM	(0.2) L
7:09 AM	(0.6) L	12:25 PM	(1.2) **H**	6:57 PM	(0.2) L
7:55 AM	(0.5) L	1:21 PM	(1.2) **H**	7:43 PM	(0.2) L
8:34 AM	(0.5) L	2:10 PM	(1.2) **H**	8:23 PM	(0.2) L
9:10 AM	(0.4) L	2:54 PM	(1.2) **H**	9:01 PM	(0.2) L
9:44 AM	(0.3) L	3:35 PM	(1.2) **H**	9:36 PM	(0.3) L
10:16 AM	(0.3) L	4:13 PM	(1.2) **H**	10:09 PM	(0.3) L

Port Phillip Heads

Day	Date		Tide 1
Sat	1		4:25 AM (1.4) **H**
Sun	2		4:52 AM (1.4) **H**
Mon	3		5:19 AM (1.3) **H**
Tue	4		5:47 AM (1.3) **H**
Wed	5		12:35 AM (0.7) L
Thu	6		1:28 AM (0.7) L
Fri	7		2:34 AM (0.8) L
Sat	8		3:54 AM (0.8) L
Sun	9	○	5:17 AM (0.7) L
Mon	10		12:24 AM (1.3) **H**
Tue	11		1:12 AM (1.4) **H**
Wed	12		1:55 AM (1.4) **H**
Thu	13		2:35 AM (1.5) **H**
Fri	14		3:14 AM (1.5) **H**
Sat	15		3:52 AM (1.5) **H**
Sun	16		4:30 AM (1.5) **H**
Mon	17		5:08 AM (1.5) **H**
Tue	18		5:49 AM (1.4) **H**
Wed	19		12:47 AM (0.6) L
Thu	20		1:44 AM (0.7) L
Fri	21		2:56 AM (0.8) L
Sat	22		4:25 AM (0.8) L
Sun	23		5:49 AM (0.7) L
Mon	24	●	12:34 AM (1.3) **H**
Tue	25		1:17 AM (1.3) **H**
Wed	26		1:53 AM (1.4) **H**
Thu	27		2:26 AM (1.4) **H**
Fri	28		2:56 AM (1.4) **H**
Sat	29		3:24 AM (1.4) **H**

POPULAR TIDE ADJUSTMENTS

Location	Adjustment
Altona	+3hrs 25min
Anderson Inlet	+10min
Anglesea	-30min
Apollo Bay	-25min
Barwon Heads	+15min
Black Rock	+3hrs 2min
Cape Otway	-30min
Cape Patterson	0
Cape Schanack	0
Carrum	+3hrs 15min
Corinella	+1hr 8min
Cnr Inlet Ent.	+25min
Cowes	+1hr 15min
Dromana	+3hrs 20min
Flinders	+48min
Frankston	+3hrs 20min
Geelong	+3hrs 30min
Golden Beach	-1hr 30min
Gunnamatta	-25min
Hastings	+1hr 15min
Hovell Pile	+3hrs 20min
Inverloch	+20min
Kilcunda	+10min
K. Is (Franklin)	-40min
K. Is(Grassy)	-10min
K. Is(Surprise Bay)	-40min
Lake Tyers	-2hrs 57min
Lakes Entrance	-2hrs 50min
Lang Lang	+1hr 55min
Lochspot	-1hr 30min
Lorne	-20min
Mahers Landing	+1hr 30min
Mallacoota Inlet	-2hrs 38min
Maribynong Riv'	+3hrs 15min
McLoughins	+2hrs 25min
McLoughlins Bch	-1hr
Melbourne	+3hrs 30min
Mordialloc	+3hrs 5min
Mornington	+3hrs 20min
New Haven	+1hr 25min
No. 1 W Ch (Annulus)	+50min
No. 2 S Ch Light	+1hr 10min
No. 8 S Ch Light	+2hrs 30min
Point Cook	+3hrs 10min
Port Albert Pier	+1hr 30min
Port Fairy	-51min
Port Phillip Hds	0
Rabbit Island	+10min
Port Welshpool Pier	+1hr 21min
Portland	-50min
Portlarington	+3hrs 15min
Portsea	+1hr 20min
Queenscliff	+35min
Refuge Cove	+ 36min
Rhyll	+1hr
Rip Bank	-15min
Rosebud	+3hrs 20min
Rye	+3hrs
Sandringham	+3hrs 20min
Seal Rock	0
Seaspray	-3hrs 11min
Shallow Inlet	+13min
Singapore Deep	- 25min
Sorrento	+2hrs 15min
S. Ch Pile Light	+3hrs 10min
St Kilda	+3hrs 20min
St Leonards	+3hrs 15min
Stony Point	+1hr
Swan Island Dock	+2hrs
Tarwin River	+3hrs
Tooradin	+1hr 45min
Venus Bay	0
Warratah Bay	0
Warrnambool	-59min
Welshpool Pier	+1hr 30min
Werribee River	+3hrs 15min
W. Ch Pile Light	+3hrs 10min
Williamstown	+3hrs 25min
Woolami	0

During Daylight Savings Time add one hour to the times stated below.

FEBRUARY 2020

Tide 2		Tide 3		Tide 4	
10:47 AM	(0.3) L	4:52 PM	(1.2) **H**	10:42 PM	(0.4) L
11:18 AM	(0.3) L	5:32 PM	(1.2) **H**	11:16 PM	(0.5) L
11:51 AM	(0.3) L	6:15 PM	(1.2) **H**	11:53 PM	(0.6) L
12:28 PM	(0.3) L	7:05 PM	(1.2) **H**		
6:20 AM	(1.2) **H**	1:11 PM	(0.3) L	8:02 PM	(1.2) **H**
7:03 AM	(1.2) **H**	2:02 PM	(0.3) L	9:07 PM	(1.2) **H**
8:00 AM	(1.1) **H**	3:03 PM	(0.3) L	10:18 PM	(1.2) **H**
9:11 AM	(1.1) **H**	4:10 PM	(0.2) L	11:27 PM	(1.2) **H**
10:28 AM	(1.1) **H**	5:19 PM	(0.2) L		
6:24 AM	(0.6) L	11:42 AM	(1.2) **H**	6:22 PM	(0.2) L
7:16 AM	(0.5) L	12:49 PM	(1.2) **H**	7:19 PM	(0.1) L
8:02 AM	(0.4) L	1:49 PM	(1.3) **H**	8:10 PM	(0.1) L
8:45 AM	(0.3) L	2:44 PM	(1.4) **H**	8:57 PM	(0.2) L
9:27 AM	(0.2) L	3:36 PM	(1.5) **H**	9:43 PM	(0.2) L
10:10 AM	(0.1) L	4:26 PM	(1.5) **H**	10:27 PM	(0.3) L
10:53 AM	(0.1) L	5:17 PM	(1.5) **H**	11:11 PM	(0.4) L
11:38 AM	(0.1) L	6:10 PM	(1.4) **H**	11:57 PM	(0.5) L
12:25 PM	(0.2) L	7:06 PM	(1.3) **H**		
6:33 AM	(1.3) **H**	1:17 PM	(0.2) L	8:08 PM	(1.3) **H**
7:25 AM	(1.2) **H**	2:15 PM	(0.3) L	9:18 PM	(1.2) **H**
8:27 AM	(1.2) **H**	3:21 PM	(0.3) L	10:34 PM	(1.2) **H**
9:41 AM	(1.1) **H**	4:34 PM	(0.3) L	11:42 PM	(1.3) **H**
11:01 AM	(1.1) **H**	5:42 PM	(0.3) L		
6:46 AM	(0.6) L	12:12 PM	(1.1) **H**	6:38 PM	(0.3) L
7:30 AM	(0.5) L	1:10 PM	(1.2) **H**	7:25 PM	(0.3) L
8:07 AM	(0.4) L	1:57 PM	(1.2) **H**	8:05 PM	(0.3) L
8:41 AM	(0.3) L	2:38 PM	(1.3) **H**	8:42 PM	(0.3) L
9:12 AM	(0.3) L	3:16 PM	(1.3) **H**	9:17 PM	(0.3) L
9:42 AM	(0.2) L	3:53 PM	(1.3) **H**	9:50 PM	(0.4) L

Port Phillip Heads

Day	Date		Tide 1
Sun	1		3:51 AM (1.4) **H**
Mon	2		4:17 AM (1.4) **H**
Tue	3		4:42 AM (1.3) **H**
Wed	4		5:09 AM (1.3) **H**
Thu	5		12:06 AM (0.7) L
Fri	6		12:53 AM (0.7) L
Sat	7		1:55 AM (0.8) L
Sun	8		3:13 AM (0.8) L
Mon	9		4:37 AM (0.7) L
Tue	10	○	5:51 AM (0.6) L
Wed	11		12:41 AM (1.3) **H**
Thu	12		1:27 AM (1.4) **H**
Fri	13		2:09 AM (1.5) **H**
Sat	14		2:49 AM (1.5) **H**
Sun	15		3:28 AM (1.5) **H**
Mon	16		4:06 AM (1.5) **H**
Tue	17		4:45 AM (1.5) **H**
Wed	18		5:25 AM (1.4) **H**
Thu	19		12:27 AM (0.7) L
Fri	20		1:20 AM (0.7) L
Sat	21		2:25 AM (0.8) L
Sun	22		3:47 AM (0.7) L
Mon	23		5:10 AM (0.7) L
Tue	24	●	6:09 AM (0.6) L
Wed	25		12:34 AM (1.3) **H**
Thu	26		1:12 AM (1.3) **H**
Fri	27		1:46 AM (1.4) **H**
Sat	28		2:17 AM (1.4) **H**
Sun	29		2:46 AM (1.4) **H**
Mon	30		3:14 AM (1.4) **H**
Tue	31		3:41 AM (1.4) **H**

POPULAR TIDE ADJUSTMENTS

Location	Adjustment
Altona	+3hrs 25min
Anderson Inlet	+10min
Anglesea	-30min
Apollo Bay	-25min
Barwon Heads	+15min
Black Rock	+3hrs 2min
Cape Otway	-30min
Cape Patterson	0
Cape Schanack	0
Carrum	+3hrs 15min
Corinella	+1hr 8min
Cnr Inlet Ent.	+25min
Cowes	+1hr 15min
Dromana	+3hrs 20min
Flinders	+48min
Frankston	+3hrs 20min
Geelong	+3hrs 30min
Golden Beach	-1hr 30min
Gunnamatta	-25min
Hastings	+1hr 15min
Hovell Pile	+3hrs 20min
Inverloch	+20min
Kilcunda	+10min
K. Is (Franklin)	-40min
K. Is(Grassy)	-10min
K. Is(Surprise Bay)	-40min
Lake Tyers	-2hrs 57min
Lakes Entrance	-2hrs 50min
Lang Lang	+1hr 55min
Lochspot	-1hr 30min
Lorne	-20min
Mahers Landing	+1hr 30min
Mallacoota Inlet	-2hrs 38min
Maribynong Riv'	+3hrs 15min
McLoughins	+2hrs 25min
McLoughlins Bch	-1hr
Melbourne	+3hrs 30min
Mordialloc	+3hrs 5min
Mornington	+3hrs 20min
New Haven	+1hr 25min
No. 1 W Ch (Annulus)	+50min
No. 2 S Ch Light	+1hr 10min
No. 8 S Ch Light	+2hrs 30min
Point Cook	+3hrs 10min
Port Albert Pier	+1hr 30min
Port Fairy	-51min
Port Phillip Hds	0
Rabbit Island	+10min
Port Welshpool Pier	+1hr 21min
Portland	-50min
Portlarington	+3hrs 15min
Portsea	+1hr 20min
Queenscliff	+35min
Refuge Cove	+ 36min
Rhyll	+1hr
Rip Bank	-15min
Rosebud	+3hrs 20min
Rye	+3hrs
Sandringham	+3hrs 20min
Seal Rock	0
Seaspray	-3hrs 11min
Shallow Inlet	+13min
Singapore Deep	- 25min
Sorrento	+2hrs 15min
S. Ch Pile Light	+3hrs 10min
St Kilda	+3hrs 20min
St Leonards	+3hrs 15min
Stony Point	+1hr
Swan Island Dock	+2hrs
Tarwin River	+3hrs
Tooradin	+1hr 45min
Venus Bay	0
Warratah Bay	0
Warrnambool	-59min
Welshpool Pier	+1hr 30min
Werribee River	+3hrs 15min
W. Ch Pile Light	+3hrs 10min
Williamstown	+3hrs 25min
Woolami	0

During Daylight Savings Time add one hour to the times stated below.

MARCH 2020

Tide 2		Tide 3		Tide 4	
10:11 AM	(0.2) L	4:28 PM	(1.4) **H**	10:22 PM	(0.4) L
10:41 AM	(0.2) L	5:05 PM	(1.3) **H**	10:54 PM	(0.5) L
11:12 AM	(0.2) L	5:44 PM	(1.3) **H**	11:28 PM	(0.6) L
11:48 AM	(0.2) L	6:28 PM	(1.3) **H**		
5:42 AM	(1.2) **H**	12:30 PM	(0.2) L	7:20 PM	(1.2) **H**
6:26 AM	(1.2) **H**	1:21 PM	(0.3) L	8:21 PM	(1.2) **H**
7:28 AM	(1.1) **H**	2:25 PM	(0.3) L	9:31 PM	(1.2) **H**
8:49 AM	(1.1) **H**	3:40 PM	(0.3) L	10:43 PM	(1.2) **H**
10:16 AM	(1.1) **H**	4:59 PM	(0.3) L	11:48 PM	(1.2) **H**
11:37 AM	(1.2) **H**	6:10 PM	(0.3) L		
6:48 AM	(0.4) L	12:47 PM	(1.3) **H**	7:09 PM	(0.2) L
7:37 AM	(0.3) L	1:46 PM	(1.4) **H**	8:01 PM	(0.2) L
8:22 AM	(0.2) L	2:38 PM	(1.5) **H**	8:48 PM	(0.3) L
9:05 AM	(0.1) L	3:28 PM	(1.6) **H**	9:32 PM	(0.3) L
9:48 AM	(0.1) L	4:15 PM	(1.6) **H**	10:15 PM	(0.4) L
10:30 AM	(0.1) L	5:02 PM	(1.6) **H**	10:57 PM	(0.5) L
11:14 AM	(0.1) L	5:50 PM	(1.5) **H**	11:40 PM	(0.6) L
11:58 AM	(0.2) L	6:40 PM	(1.4) **H**		
6:09 AM	(1.3) **H**	12:46 PM	(0.3) L	7:34 PM	(1.3) **H**
7:00 AM	(1.2) **H**	1:41 PM	(0.4) L	8:35 PM	(1.2) **H**
8:04 AM	(1.1) **H**	2:44 PM	(0.4) L	9:44 PM	(1.2) **H**
9:22 AM	(1.1) **H**	3:58 PM	(0.5) L	10:53 PM	(1.2) **H**
10:46 AM	(1.1) **H**	5:13 PM	(0.5) L	11:49 PM	(1.2) **H**
11:58 AM	(1.2) **H**	6:13 PM	(0.5) L		
6:53 AM	(0.5) L	12:53 PM	(1.2) **H**	7:02 PM	(0.4) L
7:29 AM	(0.4) L	1:37 PM	(1.3) **H**	7:43 PM	(0.4) L
8:03 AM	(0.3) L	2:17 PM	(1.4) **H**	8:21 PM	(0.4) L
8:34 AM	(0.3) L	2:54 PM	(1.4) **H**	8:56 PM	(0.4) L
9:05 AM	(0.2) L	3:29 PM	(1.5) **H**	9:29 PM	(0.5) L
9:35 AM	(0.2) L	4:04 PM	(1.5) **H**	10:01 PM	(0.5) L
10:05 AM	(0.2) L	4:40 PM	(1.5) **H**	10:34 PM	(0.6) L

Port Phillip Heads

Day	Date		Tide 1
Wed	1		4:08 AM (1.3) **H**
Thu	2		4:39 AM (1.3) **H**
Fri	3		5:17 AM (1.3) **H**
Sat	4		12:33 AM (0.7) L
Sun	5		1:33 AM (0.7) L
Mon	6		2:47 AM (0.7) L
Tue	7		4:06 AM (0.6) L
Wed	8	○	5:18 AM (0.5) L
Thu	9		12:01 AM (1.3) **H**
Fri	10		12:51 AM (1.4) **H**
Sat	11		1:37 AM (1.5) **H**
Sun	12		2:20 AM (1.5) **H**
Mon	13		3:02 AM (1.5) **H**
Tue	14		3:43 AM (1.5) **H**
Wed	15		4:23 AM (1.4) **H**
Thu	16		5:05 AM (1.4) **H**
Fri	17		12:11 AM (0.7) L
Sat	18		1:01 AM (0.7) L
Sun	19		2:00 AM (0.7) L
Mon	20		3:09 AM (0.7) L
Tue	21		4:19 AM (0.6) L
Wed	22		5:18 AM (0.6) L
Thu	23	●	6:04 AM (0.5) L
Fri	24		12:18 AM (1.3) **H**
Sat	25		12:56 AM (1.3) **H**
Sun	26		1:31 AM (1.4) **H**
Mon	27		2:04 AM (1.4) **H**
Tue	28		2:35 AM (1.4) **H**
Wed	29		3:07 AM (1.4) **H**
Thu	30		3:41 AM (1.3) **H**

POPULAR TIDE ADJUSTMENTS

Location	Adjustment
Altona	+3hrs 25min
Anderson Inlet	+10min
Anglesea	-30min
Apollo Bay	-25min
Barwon Heads	+15min
Black Rock	+3hrs 2min
Cape Otway	-30min
Cape Patterson	0
Cape Schanack	0
Carrum	+3hrs 15min
Corinella	+1hr 8min
Cnr Inlet Ent.	+25min
Cowes	+1hr 15min
Dromana	+3hrs 20min
Flinders	+48min
Frankston	+3hrs 20min
Geelong	+3hrs 30min
Golden Beach	-1hr 30min
Gunnamatta	-25min
Hastings	+1hr 15min
Hovell Pile	+3hrs 20min
Inverloch	+20min
Kilcunda	+10min
K. Is (Franklin)	-40min
K. Is(Grassy)	-10min
K. Is(Surprise Bay)	-40min
Lake Tyers	-2hrs 57min
Lakes Entrance	-2hrs 50min
Lang Lang	+1hr 55min
Lochspot	-1hr 30min
Lorne	-20min
Mahers Landing	+1hr 30min
Mallacoota Inlet	-2hrs 38min
Maribynong Riv'	+3hrs 15min
McLoughins	+2hrs 25min
McLoughlins Bch	-1hr
Melbourne	+3hrs 30min
Mordialloc	+3hrs 5min
Mornington	+3hrs 20min
New Haven	+1hr 25min
No. 1 W Ch (Annulus)	+50min
No. 2 S Ch Light	+1hr 10min
No. 8 S Ch Light	+2hrs 30min
Point Cook	+3hrs 10min
Port Albert Pier	+1hr 30min
Port Fairy	-51min
Port Phillip Hds	0
Rabbit Island	+10min
Port Welshpool Pier	+1hr 21min
Portland	-50min
Portlarington	+3hrs 15min
Portsea	+1hr 20min
Queenscliff	+35min
Refuge Cove	+ 36min
Rhyll	+1hr
Rip Bank	-15min
Rosebud	+3hrs 20min
Rye	+3hrs
Sandringham	+3hrs 20min
Seal Rock	0
Seaspray	-3hrs 11min
Shallow Inlet	+13min
Singapore Deep	- 25min
Sorrento	+2hrs 15min
S. Ch Pile Light	+3hrs 10min
St Kilda	+3hrs 20min
St Leonards	+3hrs 15min
Stony Point	+1hr
Swan Island Dock	+2hrs
Tarwin River	+3hrs
Tooradin	+1hr 45min
Venus Bay	0
Warratah Bay	0
Warrnambool	-59min
Welshpool Pier	+1hr 30min
Werribee River	+3hrs 15min
W. Ch Pile Light	+3hrs 10min
Williamstown	+3hrs 25min
Woolami	0

During Daylight Savings Time add one hour to the times stated below.

APRIL 2020

Tide 2		Tide 3		Tide 4	
10:38 AM	(0.2) L	5:17 PM	(1.4) **H**	11:07 PM	(0.6) L
11:15 AM	(0.2) L	5:59 PM	(1.4) **H**	11:46 PM	(0.7) L
11:58 AM	(0.3) L	6:47 PM	(1.3) **H**		
6:08 AM	(1.2) **H**	12:52 PM	(0.3) L	7:44 PM	(1.2) **H**
7:19 AM	(1.2) **H**	1:59 PM	(0.4) L	8:49 PM	(1.2) **H**
8:45 AM	(1.2) **H**	3:17 PM	(0.4) L	9:58 PM	(1.2) **H**
10:13 AM	(1.2) **H**	4:40 PM	(0.5) L	11:04 PM	(1.3) **H**
11:33 AM	(1.3) **H**	5:54 PM	(0.4) L		
6:18 AM	(0.3) L	12:41 PM	(1.5) **H**	6:55 PM	(0.4) L
7:09 AM	(0.2) L	1:37 PM	(1.6) **H**	7:48 PM	(0.4) L
7:57 AM	(0.1) L	2:28 PM	(1.7) **H**	8:35 PM	(0.4) L
8:42 AM	(0.1) L	3:15 PM	(1.7) **H**	9:19 PM	(0.5) L
9:25 AM	(0.1) L	4:01 PM	(1.7) **H**	10:01 PM	(0.5) L
10:07 AM	(0.1) L	4:45 PM	(1.6) **H**	10:44 PM	(0.6) L
10:49 AM	(0.2) L	5:29 PM	(1.5) **H**	11:26 PM	(0.6) L
11:32 AM	(0.3) L	6:14 PM	(1.5) **H**		
5:51 AM	(1.3) **H**	12:17 PM	(0.4) L	7:01 PM	(1.4) **H**
6:45 AM	(1.2) **H**	1:07 PM	(0.5) L	7:52 PM	(1.3) **H**
7:50 AM	(1.1) **H**	2:06 PM	(0.6) L	8:49 PM	(1.2) **H**
9:07 AM	(1.1) **H**	3:16 PM	(0.6) L	9:49 PM	(1.2) **H**
10:27 AM	(1.1) **H**	4:31 PM	(0.6) L	10:46 PM	(1.2) **H**
11:35 AM	(1.2) **H**	5:38 PM	(0.6) L	11:35 PM	(1.3) **H**
12:28 PM	(1.3) **H**	6:31 PM	(0.6) L		
6:43 AM	(0.4) L	1:12 PM	(1.4) **H**	7:15 PM	(0.6) L
7:19 AM	(0.3) L	1:51 PM	(1.5) **H**	7:55 PM	(0.6) L
7:53 AM	(0.3) L	2:29 PM	(1.5) **H**	8:32 PM	(0.6) L
8:26 AM	(0.2) L	3:05 PM	(1.6) **H**	9:08 PM	(0.6) L
8:59 AM	(0.2) L	3:41 PM	(1.6) **H**	9:42 PM	(0.6) L
9:33 AM	(0.2) L	4:17 PM	(1.6) **H**	10:16 PM	(0.6) L
10:10 AM	(0.2) L	4:54 PM	(1.5) **H**	10:52 PM	(0.6) L

Port Phillip Heads

POPULAR TIDE ADJUSTMENTS

Location	Adjustment
Altona	+3hrs 25min
Anderson Inlet	+10min
Anglesea	-30min
Apollo Bay	-25min
Barwon Heads	+15min
Black Rock	+3hrs 2min
Cape Otway	-30min
Cape Patterson	0
Cape Schanack	0
Carrum	+3hrs 15min
Corinella	+1hr 8min
Cnr Inlet Ent.	+25min
Cowes	+1hr 15min
Dromana	+3hrs 20min
Flinders	+48min
Frankston	+3hrs 20min
Geelong	+3hrs 30min
Golden Beach	-1hr 30min
Gunnamatta	-25min
Hastings	+1hr 15min
Hovell Pile	+3hrs 20min
Inverloch	+20min
Kilcunda	+10min
K. Is (Franklin)	-40min
K. Is(Grassy)	-10min
K. Is(Surprise Bay)	-40min
Lake Tyers	-2hrs 57min
Lakes Entrance	-2hrs 50min
Lang Lang	+1hr 55min
Lochspot	-1hr 30min
Lorne	-20min
Mahers Landing	+1hr 30min
Mallacoota Inlet	-2hrs 38min
Maribynong Riv'	+3hrs 15min
McLoughins	+2hrs 25min
McLoughlins Bch	-1hr
Melbourne	+3hrs 30min
Mordialloc	+3hrs 5min
Mornington	+3hrs 20min
New Haven	+1hr 25min
No. 1 W Ch (Annulus)	+50min
No. 2 S Ch Light	+1hr 10min
No. 8 S Ch Light	+2hrs 30min
Point Cook	+3hrs 10min
Port Albert Pier	+1hr 30min
Port Fairy	-51min
Port Phillip Hds	0
Rabbit Island	+10min
Port Welshpool Pier	+1hr 21min
Portland	-50min
Portlarington	+3hrs 15min
Portsea	+1hr 20min
Queenscliff	+35min
Refuge Cove	+ 36min
Rhyll	+1hr
Rip Bank	-15min
Rosebud	+3hrs 20min
Rye	+3hrs
Sandringham	+3hrs 20min
Seal Rock	0
Seaspray	-3hrs 11min
Shallow Inlet	+13min
Singapore Deep	- 25min
Sorrento	+2hrs 15min
S. Ch Pile Light	+3hrs 10min
St Kilda	+3hrs 20min
St Leonards	+3hrs 15min
Stony Point	+1hr
Swan Island Dock	+2hrs
Tarwin River	+3hrs
Tooradin	+1hr 45min
Venus Bay	0
Warratah Bay	0
Warrnambool	-59min
Welshpool Pier	+1hr 30min
Werribee River	+3hrs 15min
W. Ch Pile Light	+3hrs 10min
Williamstown	+3hrs 25min
Woolami	0

Day	Date	Tide 1
Fri	1	4:19 AM (1.3) **H**
Sat	2	5:06 AM (1.3) **H**
Sun	3	12:22 AM (0.6) L
Mon	4	1:20 AM (0.6) L
Tue	5	2:28 AM (0.6) L
Wed	6	3:38 AM (0.5) L
Thu	7 ○	4:46 AM (0.4) L
Fri	8	5:47 AM (0.3) L
Sat	9	12:13 AM (1.4) **H**
Sun	10	1:04 AM (1.5) **H**
Mon	11	1:51 AM (1.5) **H**
Tue	12	2:37 AM (1.5) **H**
Wed	13	3:21 AM (1.5) **H**
Thu	14	4:06 AM (1.4) **H**
Fri	15	4:51 AM (1.3) **H**
Sat	16	5:40 AM (1.3) **H**
Sun	17	12:44 AM (0.7) L
Mon	18	1:35 AM (0.7) L
Tue	19	2:29 AM (0.6) L
Wed	20	3:26 AM (0.6) L
Thu	21	4:20 AM (0.5) L
Fri	22	5:09 AM (0.5) L
Sat	23 ●	5:53 AM (0.4) L
Sun	24	12:01 AM (1.3) **H**
Mon	25	12:43 AM (1.3) **H**
Tue	26	1:22 AM (1.3) **H**
Wed	27	2:00 AM (1.3) **H**
Thu	28	2:40 AM (1.4) **H**
Fri	29	3:23 AM (1.3) **H**
Sat	30	4:11 AM (1.3) **H**
Sun	31	5:06 AM (1.3) **H**

During Daylight Savings Time add one hour to the times stated below.

MAY 2020

Tide 2		Tide 3		Tide 4	
10:50 AM	(0.3) L	5:35 PM	(1.5) **H**	11:33 PM	(0.7) L
11:37 AM	(0.3) L	6:21 PM	(1.4) **H**		
6:07 AM	(1.3) **H**	12:33 PM	(0.4) L	7:13 PM	(1.3) **H**
7:22 AM	(1.2) **H**	1:40 PM	(0.5) L	8:12 PM	(1.3) **H**
8:46 AM	(1.3) **H**	2:57 PM	(0.6) L	9:16 PM	(1.3) **H**
10:09 AM	(1.3) **H**	4:18 PM	(0.6) L	10:19 PM	(1.3) **H**
11:25 AM	(1.5) **H**	5:33 PM	(0.6) L	11:19 PM	(1.4) **H**
12:29 PM	(1.6) **H**	6:36 PM	(0.6) L		
6:42 AM	(0.2) L	1:24 PM	(1.7) **H**	7:30 PM	(0.6) L
7:31 AM	(0.1) L	2:14 PM	(1.7) **H**	8:19 PM	(0.6) L
8:18 AM	(0.1) L	3:01 PM	(1.8) **H**	9:04 PM	(0.6) L
9:02 AM	(0.1) L	3:45 PM	(1.7) **H**	9:48 PM	(0.6) L
9:45 AM	(0.2) L	4:27 PM	(1.7) **H**	10:31 PM	(0.6) L
10:27 AM	(0.3) L	5:08 PM	(1.6) **H**	11:13 PM	(0.6) L
11:08 AM	(0.4) L	5:48 PM	(1.5) **H**	11:57 PM	(0.7) L
11:50 AM	(0.5) L	6:29 PM	(1.4) **H**		
6:34 AM	(1.2) **H**	12:36 PM	(0.6) L	7:11 PM	(1.4) **H**
7:36 AM	(1.2) **H**	1:28 PM	(0.7) L	7:57 PM	(1.3) **H**
8:45 AM	(1.2) **H**	2:30 PM	(0.7) L	8:47 PM	(1.3) **H**
9:56 AM	(1.2) **H**	3:39 PM	(0.8) L	9:39 PM	(1.3) **H**
11:01 AM	(1.3) **H**	4:49 PM	(0.8) L	10:30 PM	(1.3) **H**
11:55 AM	(1.4) **H**	5:50 PM	(0.8) L	11:17 PM	(1.3) **H**
12:42 PM	(1.5) **H**	6:42 PM	(0.7) L		
6:34 AM	(0.3) L	1:24 PM	(1.5) **H**	7:27 PM	(0.7) L
7:13 AM	(0.3) L	2:04 PM	(1.6) **H**	8:07 PM	(0.7) L
7:51 AM	(0.2) L	2:42 PM	(1.6) **H**	8:45 PM	(0.7) L
8:29 AM	(0.2) L	3:19 PM	(1.6) **H**	9:22 PM	(0.7) L
9:08 AM	(0.2) L	3:56 PM	(1.6) **H**	9:59 PM	(0.6) L
9:49 AM	(0.2) L	4:34 PM	(1.6) **H**	10:39 PM	(0.6) L
10:34 AM	(0.3) L	5:14 PM	(1.5) **H**	11:22 PM	(0.6) L
11:23 AM	(0.4) L	5:58 PM	(1.5) **H**		

POPULAR TIDE ADJUSTMENTS

Location	Adjustment
Altona	+3hrs 25min
Anderson Inlet	+10min
Anglesea	-30min
Apollo Bay	-25min
Barwon Heads	+15min
Black Rock	+3hrs 2min
Cape Otway	-30min
Cape Patterson	0
Cape Schanack	0
Carrum	+3hrs 15min
Corinella	+1hr 8min
Cnr Inlet Ent.	+25min
Cowes	+1hr 15min
Dromana	+3hrs 20min
Flinders	+48min
Frankston	+3hrs 20min
Geelong	+3hrs 30min
Golden Beach	-1hr 30min
Gunnamatta	-25min
Hastings	+1hr 15min
Hovell Pile	+3hrs 20min
Inverloch	+20min
Kilcunda	+10min
K. Is (Franklin)	-40min
K. Is(Grassy)	-10min
K. Is(Surprise Bay)	-40min
Lake Tyers	-2hrs 57min
Lakes Entrance	-2hrs 50min
Lang Lang	+1hr 55min
Lochspot	-1hr 30min
Lorne	-20min
Mahers Landing	+1hr 30min
Mallacoota Inlet	-2hrs 38min
Maribynong Riv'	+3hrs 15min
McLoughins	+2hrs 25min
McLoughlins Bch	-1hr
Melbourne	+3hrs 30min
Mordialloc	+3hrs 5min
Mornington	+3hrs 20min
New Haven	+1hr 25min
No. 1 W Ch (Annulus)	+50min
No. 2 S Ch Light	+1hr 10min
No. 8 S Ch Light	+2hrs 30min
Point Cook	+3hrs 10min
Port Albert Pier	+1hr 30min
Port Fairy	-51min
Port Phillip Hds	0
Rabbit Island	+10min
Port Welshpool Pier	+1hr 21min
Portland	-50min
Portlarington	+3hrs 15min
Portsea	+1hr 20min
Queenscliff	+35min
Refuge Cove	+ 36min
Rhyll	+1hr
Rip Bank	-15min
Rosebud	+3hrs 20min
Rye	+3hrs
Sandringham	+3hrs 20min
Seal Rock	0
Seaspray	-3hrs 11min
Shallow Inlet	+13min
Singapore Deep	- 25min
Sorrento	+2hrs 15min
S. Ch Pile Light	+3hrs 10min
St Kilda	+3hrs 20min
St Leonards	+3hrs 15min
Stony Point	+1hr
Swan Island Dock	+2hrs
Tarwin River	+3hrs
Tooradin	+1hr 45min
Venus Bay	0
Warratah Bay	0
Warrnambool	-59min
Welshpool Pier	+1hr 30min
Werribee River	+3hrs 15min
W. Ch Pile Light	+3hrs 10min
Williamstown	+3hrs 25min
Woolami	0

Port Phillip Heads

Day	Date		Tide 1
Mon	1		12:11 AM (0.6) L
Tue	2		1:07 AM (0.5) L
Wed	3		2:08 AM (0.5) L
Thu	4		3:12 AM (0.4) L
Fri	5		4:17 AM (0.3) L
Sat	6	○	5:19 AM (0.2) L
Sun	7		6:16 AM (0.2) L
Mon	8		12:33 AM (1.5) **H**
Tue	9		1:26 AM (1.5) **H**
Wed	10		2:16 AM (1.4) **H**
Thu	11		3:05 AM (1.4) **H**
Fri	12		3:52 AM (1.4) **H**
Sat	13		4:39 AM (1.3) **H**
Sun	14		5:27 AM (1.3) **H**
Mon	15		12:19 AM (0.6) L
Tue	16		1:02 AM (0.6) L
Wed	17		1:47 AM (0.5) L
Thu	18		2:35 AM (0.5) L
Fri	19		3:25 AM (0.5) L
Sat	20		4:15 AM (0.4) L
Sun	21	●	5:05 AM (0.4) L
Mon	22		5:53 AM (0.3) L
Tue	23		6:39 AM (0.2) L
Wed	24		12:47 AM (1.3) **H**
Thu	25		1:36 AM (1.3) **H**
Fri	26		2:24 AM (1.3) **H**
Sat	27		3:15 AM (1.4) **H**
Sun	28		4:09 AM (1.4) **H**
Mon	29		5:07 AM (1.4) **H**
Tue	30		6:09 AM (1.4) **H**

During Daylight Savings Time add one hour to the times stated below.

JUNE 2020

Tide 2		Tide 3		Tide 4	
6:11 AM	(1.3) **H**	12:19 PM	(0.5) L	6:46 PM	(1.4) **H**
7:24 AM	(1.3) **H**	1:24 PM	(0.6) L	7:40 PM	(1.4) **H**
8:40 AM	(1.4) **H**	2:35 PM	(0.7) L	8:38 PM	(1.4) **H**
9:58 AM	(1.4) **H**	3:52 PM	(0.7) L	9:38 PM	(1.4) **H**
11:10 AM	(1.5) **H**	5:07 PM	(0.8) L	10:38 PM	(1.4) **H**
12:14 PM	(1.6) **H**	6:14 PM	(0.7) L	11:37 PM	(1.4) **H**
1:09 PM	(1.7) **H**	7:12 PM	(0.7) L		
7:08 AM	(0.2) L	1:59 PM	(1.7) **H**	8:03 PM	(0.7) L
7:57 AM	(0.2) L	2:44 PM	(1.7) **H**	8:50 PM	(0.6) L
8:42 AM	(0.2) L	3:27 PM	(1.7) **H**	9:34 PM	(0.6) L
9:25 AM	(0.2) L	4:07 PM	(1.7) **H**	10:16 PM	(0.6) L
10:06 AM	(0.3) L	4:44 PM	(1.6) **H**	10:57 PM	(0.6) L
10:45 AM	(0.4) L	5:20 PM	(1.5) **H**	11:38 PM	(0.6) L
11:24 AM	(0.5) L	5:55 PM	(1.5) **H**		
6:18 AM	(1.2) **H**	12:05 PM	(0.6) L	6:31 PM	(1.4) **H**
7:13 AM	(1.2) **H**	12:51 PM	(0.7) L	7:10 PM	(1.4) **H**
8:13 AM	(1.2) **H**	1:45 PM	(0.8) L	7:52 PM	(1.3) **H**
9:15 AM	(1.2) **H**	2:46 PM	(0.8) L	8:38 PM	(1.3) **H**
10:18 AM	(1.3) **H**	3:54 PM	(0.9) L	9:28 PM	(1.3) **H**
11:17 AM	(1.4) **H**	5:02 PM	(0.9) L	10:19 PM	(1.3) **H**
12:09 PM	(1.4) **H**	6:04 PM	(0.8) L	11:09 PM	(1.3) **H**
12:56 PM	(1.5) **H**	6:56 PM	(0.8) L	11:59 PM	(1.3) **H**
1:39 PM	(1.6) **H**	7:41 PM	(0.7) L		
7:23 AM	(0.2) L	2:19 PM	(1.6) **H**	8:23 PM	(0.7) L
8:08 AM	(0.2) L	2:58 PM	(1.6) **H**	9:02 PM	(0.6) L
8:52 AM	(0.2) L	3:36 PM	(1.6) **H**	9:42 PM	(0.6) L
9:37 AM	(0.3) L	4:14 PM	(1.6) **H**	10:24 PM	(0.5) L
10:23 AM	(0.3) L	4:53 PM	(1.5) **H**	11:08 PM	(0.5) L
11:13 AM	(0.4) L	5:34 PM	(1.5) **H**	11:56 PM	(0.4) L
12:06 PM	(0.5) L	6:19 PM	(1.5) **H**		

POPULAR TIDE ADJUSTMENTS

Location	Adjustment
Altona	+3hrs 25min
Anderson Inlet	+10min
Anglesea	-30min
Apollo Bay	-25min
Barwon Heads	+15min
Black Rock	+3hrs 2min
Cape Otway	-30min
Cape Patterson	0
Cape Schanack	0
Carrum	+3hrs 15min
Corinella	+1hr 8min
Cnr Inlet Ent.	+25min
Cowes	+1hr 15min
Dromana	+3hrs 20min
Flinders	+48min
Frankston	+3hrs 20min
Geelong	+3hrs 30min
Golden Beach	-1hr 30min
Gunnamatta	-25min
Hastings	+1hr 15min
Hovell Pile	+3hrs 20min
Inverloch	+20min
Kilcunda	+10min
K. Is (Franklin)	-40min
K. Is(Grassy)	-10min
K. Is(Surprise Bay)	-40min
Lake Tyers	-2hrs 57min
Lakes Entrance	-2hrs 50min
Lang Lang	+1hr 55min
Lochspot	-1hr 30min
Lorne	-20min
Mahers Landing	+1hr 30min
Mallacoota Inlet	-2hrs 38min
Maribynong Riv'	+3hrs 15min
McLoughins	+2hrs 25min
McLoughlins Bch	-1hr
Melbourne	+3hrs 30min
Mordialloc	+3hrs 5min
Mornington	+3hrs 20min
New Haven	+1hr 25min
No. 1 W Ch (Annulus)	+50min
No. 2 S Ch Light	+1hr 10min
No. 8 S Ch Light	+2hrs 30min
Point Cook	+3hrs 10min
Port Albert Pier	+1hr 30min
Port Fairy	-51min
Port Phillip Hds	0
Rabbit Island	+10min
Port Welshpool Pier	+1hr 21min
Portland	-50min
Portlarington	+3hrs 15min
Portsea	+1hr 20min
Queenscliff	+35min
Refuge Cove	+ 36min
Rhyll	+1hr
Rip Bank	-15min
Rosebud	+3hrs 20min
Rye	+3hrs
Sandringham	+3hrs 20min
Seal Rock	0
Seaspray	-3hrs 11min
Shallow Inlet	+13min
Singapore Deep	- 25min
Sorrento	+2hrs 15min
S. Ch Pile Light	+3hrs 10min
St Kilda	+3hrs 20min
St Leonards	+3hrs 15min
Stony Point	+1hr
Swan Island Dock	+2hrs
Tarwin River	+3hrs
Tooradin	+1hr 45min
Venus Bay	0
Warratah Bay	0
Warrnambool	-59min
Welshpool Pier	+1hr 30min
Werribee River	+3hrs 15min
W. Ch Pile Light	+3hrs 10min
Williamstown	+3hrs 25min
Woolami	0

Port Phillip Heads

Day	Date		Tide 1	
Wed	1		12:48 AM	(0.4) L
Thu	2		1:45 AM	(0.3) L
Fri	3		2:46 AM	(0.3) L
Sat	4		3:50 AM	(0.3) L
Sun	5	○	4:53 AM	(0.2) L
Mon	6		5:54 AM	(0.2) L
Tue	7		12:09 AM	(1.4) **H**
Wed	8		1:08 AM	(1.4) **H**
Thu	9		2:02 AM	(1.4) **H**
Fri	10		2:52 AM	(1.4) **H**
Sat	11		3:38 AM	(1.3) **H**
Sun	12		4:23 AM	(1.3) **H**
Mon	13		5:08 AM	(1.3) **H**
Tue	14		5:53 AM	(1.2) **H**
Wed	15		12:23 AM	(0.5) L
Thu	16		1:03 AM	(0.5) L
Fri	17		1:46 AM	(0.4) L
Sat	18		2:34 AM	(0.4) L
Sun	19		3:27 AM	(0.4) L
Mon	20		4:22 AM	(0.3) L
Tue	21	●	5:18 AM	(0.3) L
Wed	22		6:13 AM	(0.2) L
Thu	23		12:27 AM	(1.3) **H**
Fri	24		1:24 AM	(1.3) **H**
Sat	25		2:19 AM	(1.4) **H**
Sun	26		3:12 AM	(1.4) **H**
Mon	27		4:06 AM	(1.4) **H**
Tue	28		5:01 AM	(1.4) **H**
Wed	29		5:59 AM	(1.4) **H**
Thu	30		12:25 AM	(0.3) L
Fri	31		1:19 AM	(0.3) L

During Daylight Savings Time add one hour to the times stated below.

JULY 2020

Tide 2		Tide 3		Tide 4	
7:16 AM	(1.4) **H**	1:05 PM	(0.7) L	7:08 PM	(1.4) **H**
8:26 AM	(1.4) **H**	2:10 PM	(0.8) L	8:03 PM	(1.4) **H**
9:39 AM	(1.4) **H**	3:23 PM	(0.8) L	9:02 PM	(1.4) **H**
10:51 AM	(1.5) **H**	4:39 PM	(0.8) L	10:04 PM	(1.4) **H**
11:56 AM	(1.5) **H**	5:52 PM	(0.8) L	11:07 PM	(1.4) **H**
12:53 PM	(1.6) **H**	6:54 PM	(0.7) L		
6:49 AM	(0.2) L	1:42 PM	(1.6) **H**	7:46 PM	(0.7) L
7:39 AM	(0.2) L	2:26 PM	(1.6) **H**	8:33 PM	(0.6) L
8:24 AM	(0.2) L	3:06 PM	(1.6) **H**	9:16 PM	(0.6) L
9:06 AM	(0.3) L	3:42 PM	(1.6) **H**	9:56 PM	(0.5) L
9:45 AM	(0.4) L	4:17 PM	(1.6) **H**	10:34 PM	(0.5) L
10:23 AM	(0.4) L	4:49 PM	(1.5) **H**	11:10 PM	(0.5) L
10:59 AM	(0.5) L	5:20 PM	(1.5) **H**	11:46 PM	(0.5) L
11:36 AM	(0.6) L	5:51 PM	(1.4) **H**		
6:41 AM	(1.2) **H**	12:16 PM	(0.7) L	6:23 PM	(1.4) **H**
7:33 AM	(1.2) **H**	1:03 PM	(0.8) L	7:00 PM	(1.3) **H**
8:30 AM	(1.2) **H**	1:57 PM	(0.8) L	7:43 PM	(1.3) **H**
9:32 AM	(1.3) **H**	3:01 PM	(0.9) L	8:32 PM	(1.2) **H**
10:35 AM	(1.3) **H**	4:12 PM	(0.9) L	9:28 PM	(1.2) **H**
11:35 AM	(1.4) **H**	5:23 PM	(0.9) L	10:28 PM	(1.2) **H**
12:27 PM	(1.4) **H**	6:24 PM	(0.8) L	11:28 PM	(1.2) **H**
1:13 PM	(1.5) **H**	7:14 PM	(0.7) L		
7:04 AM	(0.2) L	1:55 PM	(1.5) **H**	7:58 PM	(0.6) L
7:54 AM	(0.2) L	2:35 PM	(1.5) **H**	8:40 PM	(0.5) L
8:41 AM	(0.2) L	3:13 PM	(1.5) **H**	9:22 PM	(0.4) L
9:27 AM	(0.3) L	3:51 PM	(1.5) **H**	10:04 PM	(0.4) L
10:13 AM	(0.3) L	4:29 PM	(1.5) **H**	10:48 PM	(0.3) L
11:01 AM	(0.4) L	5:09 PM	(1.5) **H**	11:35 PM	(0.3) L
11:50 AM	(0.6) L	5:52 PM	(1.5) **H**		
6:59 AM	(1.4) **H**	12:44 PM	(0.7) L	6:38 PM	(1.4) **H**
8:05 AM	(1.4) **H**	1:44 PM	(0.8) L	7:31 PM	(1.4) H

Port Phillip Heads

Day	Date		Tide 1
Sat	1		2:19 AM (0.3) L
Sun	2		3:23 AM (0.3) L
Mon	3		4:31 AM (0.3) L
Tue	4	○	5:35 AM (0.3) L
Wed	5		6:33 AM (0.3) L
Thu	6		12:57 AM (1.3) **H**
Fri	7		1:51 AM (1.3) **H**
Sat	8		2:38 AM (1.3) **H**
Sun	9		3:22 AM (1.3) **H**
Mon	10		4:02 AM (1.3) **H**
Tue	11		4:42 AM (1.3) **H**
Wed	12		5:22 AM (1.3) **H**
Thu	13		6:04 AM (1.3) **H**
Fri	14		12:16 AM (0.4) L
Sat	15		12:57 AM (0.4) L
Sun	16		1:46 AM (0.4) L
Mon	17		2:42 AM (0.3) L
Tue	18		3:46 AM (0.3) L
Wed	19	●	4:52 AM (0.3) L
Thu	20		5:55 AM (0.3) L
Fri	21		12:20 AM (1.3) **H**
Sat	22		1:20 AM (1.4) **H**
Sun	23		2:15 AM (1.4) **H**
Mon	24		3:07 AM (1.5) **H**
Tue	25		3:58 AM (1.5) **H**
Wed	26		4:49 AM (1.5) **H**
Thu	27		5:42 AM (1.5) **H**
Fri	28		6:38 AM (1.4) **H**
Sat	29		12:51 AM (0.2) L
Sun	30		1:50 AM (0.3) L
Mon	31		2:56 AM (0.3) L

POPULAR TIDE ADJUSTMENTS

Location	Adjustment
Altona	+3hrs 25min
Anderson Inlet	+10min
Anglesea	-30min
Apollo Bay	-25min
Barwon Heads	+15min
Black Rock	+3hrs 2min
Cape Otway	-30min
Cape Patterson	0
Cape Schanack	0
Carrum	+3hrs 15min
Corinella	+1hr 8min
Cnr Inlet Ent.	+25min
Cowes	+1hr 15min
Dromana	+3hrs 20min
Flinders	+48min
Frankston	+3hrs 20min
Geelong	+3hrs 30min
Golden Beach	-1hr 30min
Gunnamatta	-25min
Hastings	+1hr 15min
Hovell Pile	+3hrs 20min
Inverloch	+20min
Kilcunda	+10min
K. Is (Franklin)	-40min
K. Is(Grassy)	-10min
K. Is(Surprise Bay)	-40min
Lake Tyers	-2hrs 57min
Lakes Entrance	-2hrs 50min
Lang Lang	+1hr 55min
Lochspot	-1hr 30min
Lorne	-20min
Mahers Landing	+1hr 30min
Mallacoota Inlet	-2hrs 38min
Maribynong Riv'	+3hrs 15min
McLoughins	+2hrs 25min
McLoughlins Bch	-1hr
Melbourne	+3hrs 30min
Mordialloc	+3hrs 5min
Mornington	+3hrs 20min
New Haven	+1hr 25min
No. 1 W Ch (Annulus)	+50min
No. 2 S Ch Light	+1hr 10min
No. 8 S Ch Light	+2hrs 30min
Point Cook	+3hrs 10min
Port Albert Pier	+1hr 30min
Port Fairy	-51min
Port Phillip Hds	0
Rabbit Island	+10min
Port Welshpool Pier	+1hr 21min
Portland	-50min
Portlarington	+3hrs 15min
Portsea	+1hr 20min
Queenscliff	+35min
Refuge Cove	+ 36min
Rhyll	+1hr
Rip Bank	-15min
Rosebud	+3hrs 20min
Rye	+3hrs
Sandringham	+3hrs 20min
Seal Rock	0
Seaspray	-3hrs 11min
Shallow Inlet	+13min
Singapore Deep	- 25min
Sorrento	+2hrs 15min
S. Ch Pile Light	+3hrs 10min
St Kilda	+3hrs 20min
St Leonards	+3hrs 15min
Stony Point	+1hr
Swan Island Dock	+2hrs
Tarwin River	+3hrs
Tooradin	+1hr 45min
Venus Bay	0
Warratah Bay	0
Warrnambool	-59min
Welshpool Pier	+1hr 30min
Werribee River	+3hrs 15min
W. Ch Pile Light	+3hrs 10min
Williamstown	+3hrs 25min
Woolami	0

During Daylight Savings Time add one hour to the times stated below.

AUGUST 2020

Tide 2		Tide 3		Tide 4	
9:15 AM	(1.4) **H**	2:54 PM	(0.8) L	8:31 PM	(1.3) **H**
10:29 AM	(1.4) **H**	4:13 PM	(0.8) L	9:37 PM	(1.3) **H**
11:36 AM	(1.4) **H**	5:32 PM	(0.8) L	10:47 PM	(1.3) **H**
12:33 PM	(1.5) **H**	6:36 PM	(0.7) L	11:56 PM	(1.3) **H**
1:21 PM	(1.5) **H**	7:27 PM	(0.6) L		
7:23 AM	(0.3) L	2:02 PM	(1.5) **H**	8:11 PM	(0.5) L
8:08 AM	(0.3) L	2:39 PM	(1.5) **H**	8:51 PM	(0.5) L
8:48 AM	(0.3) L	3:13 PM	(1.5) **H**	9:27 PM	(0.4) L
9:25 AM	(0.4) L	3:44 PM	(1.5) **H**	10:01 PM	(0.4) L
9:59 AM	(0.4) L	4:13 PM	(1.5) **H**	10:34 PM	(0.4) L
10:33 AM	(0.5) L	4:41 PM	(1.4) **H**	11:07 PM	(0.4) L
11:07 AM	(0.6) L	5:09 PM	(1.4) **H**	11:40 PM	(0.4) L
11:44 AM	(0.7) L	5:38 PM	(1.3) **H**		
6:51 AM	(1.3) **H**	12:24 PM	(0.7) L	6:11 PM	(1.3) **H**
7:44 AM	(1.2) **H**	1:14 PM	(0.8) L	6:51 PM	(1.2) **H**
8:45 AM	(1.2) **H**	2:14 PM	(0.8) L	7:44 PM	(1.2) **H**
9:51 AM	(1.2) **H**	3:26 PM	(0.8) L	8:50 PM	(1.2) **H**
10:57 AM	(1.3) **H**	4:43 PM	(0.8) L	10:02 PM	(1.2) **H**
11:55 AM	(1.3) **H**	5:51 PM	(0.7) L	11:14 PM	(1.2) **H**
12:45 PM	(1.4) **H**	6:45 PM	(0.6) L		
6:52 AM	(0.2) L	1:28 PM	(1.4) **H**	7:32 PM	(0.5) L
7:44 AM	(0.2) L	2:08 PM	(1.5) **H**	8:16 PM	(0.4) L
8:31 AM	(0.2) L	2:46 PM	(1.5) **H**	8:58 PM	(0.3) L
9:17 AM	(0.3) L	3:25 PM	(1.5) **H**	9:41 PM	(0.2) L
10:02 AM	(0.4) L	4:03 PM	(1.5) **H**	10:25 PM	(0.2) L
10:46 AM	(0.5) L	4:42 PM	(1.5) **H**	11:10 PM	(0.2) L
11:33 AM	(0.6) L	5:24 PM	(1.5) **H**	11:59 PM	(0.2) L
12:23 PM	(0.7) L	6:10 PM	(1.4) **H**		
7:38 AM	(1.4) **H**	1:19 PM	(0.7) L	7:04 PM	(1.3) **H**
8:46 AM	(1.3) **H**	2:27 PM	(0.8) L	8:07 PM	(1.3) **H**
9:59 AM	(1.3) **H**	3:49 PM	(0.8) L	9:20 PM	(1.2) H

Port Phillip Heads

Day	Date	Tide 1
Tue	1	4:09 AM (0.4) L
Wed	2 ○	5:19 AM (0.4) L
Thu	3	6:18 AM (0.3) L
Fri	4	12:49 AM (1.3) **H**
Sat	5	1:38 AM (1.3) **H**
Sun	6	2:21 AM (1.4) **H**
Mon	7	3:00 AM (1.4) **H**
Tue	8	3:37 AM (1.4) **H**
Wed	9	4:13 AM (1.4) **H**
Thu	10	4:50 AM (1.4) **H**
Fri	11	5:28 AM (1.3) **H**
Sat	12	6:11 AM (1.3) **H**
Sun	13	12:11 AM (0.3) L
Mon	14	1:01 AM (0.3) L
Tue	15	2:03 AM (0.4) L
Wed	16	3:16 AM (0.4) L
Thu	17 ●	4:32 AM (0.4) L
Fri	18	5:42 AM (0.3) L
Sat	19	12:18 AM (1.3) **H**
Sun	20	1:16 AM (1.5) **H**
Mon	21	2:08 AM (1.6) **H**
Tue	22	2:58 AM (1.6) **H**
Wed	23	3:46 AM (1.6) **H**
Thu	24	4:33 AM (1.6) **H**
Fri	25	5:22 AM (1.5) **H**
Sat	26	6:13 AM (1.4) **H**
Sun	27	12:23 AM (0.3) L
Mon	28	1:20 AM (0.4) L
Tue	29	2:27 AM (0.4) L
Wed	30	3:43 AM (0.5) L

POPULAR TIDE ADJUSTMENTS

Location	Adjustment
Altona	+3hrs 25min
Anderson Inlet	+10min
Anglesea	-30min
Apollo Bay	-25min
Barwon Heads	+15min
Black Rock	+3hrs 2min
Cape Otway	-30min
Cape Patterson	0
Cape Schanack	0
Carrum	+3hrs 15min
Corinella	+1hr 8min
Cnr Inlet Ent.	+25min
Cowes	+1hr 15min
Dromana	+3hrs 20min
Flinders	+48min
Frankston	+3hrs 20min
Geelong	+3hrs 30min
Golden Beach	-1hr 30min
Gunnamatta	-25min
Hastings	+1hr 15min
Hovell Pile	+3hrs 20min
Inverloch	+20min
Kilcunda	+10min
K. Is (Franklin)	-40min
K. Is(Grassy)	-10min
K. Is(Surprise Bay)	-40min
Lake Tyers	-2hrs 57min
Lakes Entrance	-2hrs 50min
Lang Lang	+1hr 55min
Lochspot	-1hr 30min
Lorne	-20min
Mahers Landing	+1hr 30min
Mallacoota Inlet	-2hrs 38min
Maribynong Riv'	+3hrs 15min
McLoughins	+2hrs 25min
McLoughlins Bch	-1hr
Melbourne	+3hrs 30min
Mordialloc	+3hrs 5min
Mornington	+3hrs 20min
New Haven	+1hr 25min
No. 1 W Ch (Annulus)	+50min
No. 2 S Ch Light	+1hr 10min
No. 8 S Ch Light	+2hrs 30min
Point Cook	+3hrs 10min
Port Albert Pier	+1hr 30min
Port Fairy	-51min
Port Phillip Hds	0
Rabbit Island	+10min
Port Welshpool Pier	+1hr 21min
Portland	-50min
Portlarington	+3hrs 15min
Portsea	+1hr 20min
Queenscliff	+35min
Refuge Cove	+ 36min
Rhyll	+1hr
Rip Bank	-15min
Rosebud	+3hrs 20min
Rye	+3hrs
Sandringham	+3hrs 20min
Seal Rock	0
Seaspray	-3hrs 11min
Shallow Inlet	+13min
Singapore Deep	- 25min
Sorrento	+2hrs 15min
S. Ch Pile Light	+3hrs 10min
St Kilda	+3hrs 20min
St Leonards	+3hrs 15min
Stony Point	+1hr
Swan Island Dock	+2hrs
Tarwin River	+3hrs
Tooradin	+1hr 45min
Venus Bay	0
Warratah Bay	0
Warrnambool	-59min
Welshpool Pier	+1hr 30min
Werribee River	+3hrs 15min
W. Ch Pile Light	+3hrs 10min
Williamstown	+3hrs 25min
Woolami	0

During Daylight Savings Time add one hour to the times stated below.

SEPTEMBER 2020

Tide 2		Tide 3		Tide 4	
11:09 AM	(1.3) **H**	5:11 PM	(0.7) L	10:38 PM	(1.2) **H**
12:06 PM	(1.3) **H**	6:15 PM	(0.6) L	11:50 PM	(1.2) **H**
12:52 PM	(1.4) **H**	7:03 PM	(0.5) L		
7:07 AM	(0.3) L	1:31 PM	(1.4) **H**	7:43 PM	(0.4) L
7:49 AM	(0.3) L	2:05 PM	(1.4) **H**	8:19 PM	(0.4) L
8:27 AM	(0.3) L	2:37 PM	(1.4) **H**	8:52 PM	(0.3) L
9:02 AM	(0.4) L	3:07 PM	(1.4) **H**	9:24 PM	(0.3) L
9:36 AM	(0.4) L	3:35 PM	(1.4) **H**	9:54 PM	(0.3) L
10:08 AM	(0.5) L	4:01 PM	(1.4) **H**	10:25 PM	(0.3) L
10:41 AM	(0.6) L	4:27 PM	(1.3) **H**	10:56 PM	(0.3) L
11:15 AM	(0.6) L	4:55 PM	(1.3) **H**	11:31 PM	(0.3) L
11:52 AM	(0.7) L	5:27 PM	(1.2) **H**		
7:01 AM	(1.2) **H**	12:38 PM	(0.7) L	6:09 PM	(1.2) **H**
7:59 AM	(1.2) **H**	1:37 PM	(0.8) L	7:09 PM	(1.1) **H**
9:06 AM	(1.2) **H**	2:49 PM	(0.8) L	8:28 PM	(1.1) **H**
10:14 AM	(1.2) **H**	4:08 PM	(0.7) L	9:52 PM	(1.1) **H**
11:17 AM	(1.2) **H**	5:19 PM	(0.6) L	11:10 PM	(1.2) **H**
12:09 PM	(1.3) **H**	6:16 PM	(0.5) L		
6:41 AM	(0.3) L	12:55 PM	(1.4) **H**	7:05 PM	(0.3) L
7:33 AM	(0.3) L	1:37 PM	(1.4) **H**	7:50 PM	(0.2) L
8:20 AM	(0.3) L	2:18 PM	(1.5) **H**	8:34 PM	(0.1) L
9:05 AM	(0.3) L	2:57 PM	(1.5) **H**	9:17 PM	(0.1) L
9:48 AM	(0.4) L	3:37 PM	(1.5) **H**	10:01 PM	(0.1) L
10:31 AM	(0.5) L	4:17 PM	(1.5) **H**	10:45 PM	(0.1) L
11:16 AM	(0.6) L	5:00 PM	(1.4) **H**	11:32 PM	(0.2) L
12:04 PM	(0.6) L	5:47 PM	(1.3) **H**		
7:09 AM	(1.3) **H**	12:59 PM	(0.7) L	6:43 PM	(1.2) **H**
8:11 AM	(1.3) **H**	2:05 PM	(0.7) L	7:51 PM	(1.2) **H**
9:19 AM	(1.2) **H**	3:24 PM	(0.7) L	9:11 PM	(1.1) **H**
10:28 AM	(1.2) **H**	4:44 PM	(0.6) L	10:33 PM	(1.1) **H**

POPULAR TIDE ADJUSTMENTS

Location	Adjustment
Altona	+3hrs 25min
Anderson Inlet	+10min
Anglesea	-30min
Apollo Bay	-25min
Barwon Heads	+15min
Black Rock	+3hrs 2min
Cape Otway	-30min
Cape Patterson	0
Cape Schanack	0
Carrum	+3hrs 15min
Corinella	+1hr 8min
Cnr Inlet Ent.	+25min
Cowes	+1hr 15min
Dromana	+3hrs 20min
Flinders	+48min
Frankston	+3hrs 20min
Geelong	+3hrs 30min
Golden Beach	-1hr 30min
Gunnamatta	-25min
Hastings	+1hr 15min
Hovell Pile	+3hrs 20min
Inverloch	+20min
Kilcunda	+10min
K. Is (Franklin)	-40min
K. Is(Grassy)	-10min
K. Is(Surprise Bay)	-40min
Lake Tyers	-2hrs 57min
Lakes Entrance	-2hrs 50min
Lang Lang	+1hr 55min
Lochspot	-1hr 30min
Lorne	-20min
Mahers Landing	+1hr 30min
Mallacoota Inlet	-2hrs 38min
Maribynong Riv'	+3hrs 15min
McLoughins	+2hrs 25min
McLoughlins Bch	-1hr
Melbourne	+3hrs 30min
Mordialloc	+3hrs 5min
Mornington	+3hrs 20min
New Haven	+1hr 25min
No. 1 W Ch (Annulus)	+50min
No. 2 S Ch Light	+1hr 10min
No. 8 S Ch Light	+2hrs 30min
Point Cook	+3hrs 10min
Port Albert Pier	+1hr 30min
Port Fairy	-51min
Port Phillip Hds	0
Rabbit Island	+10min
Port Welshpool Pier	+1hr 21min
Portland	-50min
Portlarington	+3hrs 15min
Portsea	+1hr 20min
Queenscliff	+35min
Refuge Cove	+ 36min
Rhyll	+1hr
Rip Bank	-15min
Rosebud	+3hrs 20min
Rye	+3hrs
Sandringham	+3hrs 20min
Seal Rock	0
Seaspray	-3hrs 11min
Shallow Inlet	+13min
Singapore Deep	- 25min
Sorrento	+2hrs 15min
S. Ch Pile Light	+3hrs 10min
St Kilda	+3hrs 20min
St Leonards	+3hrs 15min
Stony Point	+1hr
Swan Island Dock	+2hrs
Tarwin River	+3hrs
Tooradin	+1hr 45min
Venus Bay	0
Warratah Bay	0
Warrnambool	-59min
Welshpool Pier	+1hr 30min
Werribee River	+3hrs 15min
W. Ch Pile Light	+3hrs 10min
Williamstown	+3hrs 25min
Woolami	0

Port Phillip Heads

Day	Date		Tide 1	
Thu	1		4:58 AM	(0.5) L
Fri	2	○	5:59 AM	(0.5) L
Sat	3		12:37 AM	(1.3) **H**
Sun	4		1:21 AM	(1.4) **H**
Mon	5		2:00 AM	(1.4) **H**
Tue	6		2:37 AM	(1.5) **H**
Wed	7		3:11 AM	(1.5) **H**
Thu	8		3:46 AM	(1.5) **H**
Fri	9		4:21 AM	(1.5) **H**
Sat	10		4:57 AM	(1.4) **H**
Sun	11		5:37 AM	(1.3) **H**
Mon	12		6:22 AM	(1.3) **H**
Tue	13		12:25 AM	(0.3) L
Wed	14		1:31 AM	(0.4) L
Thu	15		2:49 AM	(0.5) L
Fri	16		4:11 AM	(0.5) L
Sat	17	●	5:26 AM	(0.5) L
Sun	18		12:12 AM	(1.4) **H**
Mon	19		1:08 AM	(1.6) **H**
Tue	20		1:59 AM	(1.6) **H**
Wed	21		2:46 AM	(1.7) **H**
Thu	22		3:32 AM	(1.7) **H**
Fri	23		4:17 AM	(1.6) **H**
Sat	24		5:02 AM	(1.6) **H**
Sun	25		5:49 AM	(1.5) **H**
Mon	26		6:37 AM	(1.3) **H**
Tue	27		12:48 AM	(0.4) L
Wed	28		1:51 AM	(0.5) L
Thu	29		3:04 AM	(0.6) L
Fri	30		4:22 AM	(0.6) L
Sat	31		5:28 AM	(0.6) L

During Daylight Savings Time add one hour to the times stated below.

OCTOBER 2020

Tide 2		Tide 3		Tide 4	
11:26 AM	(1.2) **H**	5:44 PM	(0.5) L	11:43 PM	(1.2) **H**
12:12 PM	(1.3) **H**	6:29 PM	(0.4) L		
6:47 AM	(0.4) L	12:50 PM	(1.3) **H**	7:08 PM	(0.4) L
7:28 AM	(0.4) L	1:25 PM	(1.4) **H**	7:42 PM	(0.3) L
8:05 AM	(0.4) L	1:57 PM	(1.4) **H**	8:14 PM	(0.2) L
8:40 AM	(0.4) L	2:27 PM	(1.4) **H**	8:45 PM	(0.2) L
9:13 AM	(0.5) L	2:55 PM	(1.4) **H**	9:15 PM	(0.2) L
9:45 AM	(0.5) L	3:23 PM	(1.3) **H**	9:46 PM	(0.2) L
10:18 AM	(0.6) L	3:50 PM	(1.3) **H**	10:18 PM	(0.2) L
10:51 AM	(0.6) L	4:20 PM	(1.3) **H**	10:53 PM	(0.2) L
11:28 AM	(0.6) L	4:56 PM	(1.2) **H**	11:34 PM	(0.3) L
12:13 PM	(0.7) L	5:44 PM	(1.2) **H**		
7:17 AM	(1.2) **H**	1:10 PM	(0.7) L	6:54 PM	(1.1) **H**
8:20 AM	(1.2) **H**	2:21 PM	(0.7) L	8:20 PM	(1.1) **H**
9:27 AM	(1.2) **H**	3:36 PM	(0.6) L	9:48 PM	(1.2) **H**
10:32 AM	(1.2) **H**	4:46 PM	(0.5) L	11:06 PM	(1.3) **H**
11:29 AM	(1.3) **H**	5:45 PM	(0.3) L		
6:27 AM	(0.4) L	12:19 PM	(1.3) **H**	6:37 PM	(0.2) L
7:19 AM	(0.4) L	1:05 PM	(1.4) **H**	7:25 PM	(0.1) L
8:07 AM	(0.4) L	1:49 PM	(1.5) **H**	8:10 PM	(0.0) L
8:51 AM	(0.4) L	2:31 PM	(1.5) **H**	8:55 PM	(0.0) L
9:35 AM	(0.5) L	3:14 PM	(1.5) **H**	9:38 PM	(0.0) L
10:18 AM	(0.5) L	3:56 PM	(1.4) **H**	10:22 PM	(0.1) L
11:02 AM	(0.6) L	4:41 PM	(1.4) **H**	11:07 PM	(0.2) L
11:49 AM	(0.6) L	5:31 PM	(1.3) **H**	11:55 PM	(0.3) L
12:41 PM	(0.6) L	6:29 PM	(1.2) **H**		
7:31 AM	(1.3) **H**	1:42 PM	(0.6) L	7:38 PM	(1.1) **H**
8:29 AM	(1.2) **H**	2:51 PM	(0.6) L	8:58 PM	(1.1) **H**
9:30 AM	(1.2) **H**	4:02 PM	(0.6) L	10:20 PM	(1.1) **H**
10:28 AM	(1.2) **H**	5:01 PM	(0.5) L	11:26 PM	(1.2) **H**
11:17 AM	(1.2) **H**	5:47 PM	(0.4) L		

POPULAR TIDE ADJUSTMENTS

Location	Adjustment
Altona	+3hrs 25min
Anderson Inlet	+10min
Anglesea	-30min
Apollo Bay	-25min
Barwon Heads	+15min
Black Rock	+3hrs 2min
Cape Otway	-30min
Cape Patterson	0
Cape Schanack	0
Carrum	+3hrs 15min
Corinella	+1hr 8min
Cnr Inlet Ent.	+25min
Cowes	+1hr 15min
Dromana	+3hrs 20min
Flinders	+48min
Frankston	+3hrs 20min
Geelong	+3hrs 30min
Golden Beach	-1hr 30min
Gunnamatta	-25min
Hastings	+1hr 15min
Hovell Pile	+3hrs 20min
Inverloch	+20min
Kilcunda	+10min
K. Is (Franklin)	-40min
K. Is(Grassy)	-10min
K. Is(Surprise Bay)	-40min
Lake Tyers	-2hrs 57min
Lakes Entrance	-2hrs 50min
Lang Lang	+1hr 55min
Lochspot	-1hr 30min
Lorne	-20min
Mahers Landing	+1hr 30min
Mallacoota Inlet	-2hrs 38min
Maribynong Riv'	+3hrs 15min
McLoughins	+2hrs 25min
McLoughlins Bch	-1hr
Melbourne	+3hrs 30min
Mordialloc	+3hrs 5min
Mornington	+3hrs 20min
New Haven	+1hr 25min
No. 1 W Ch (Annulus)	+50min
No. 2 S Ch Light	+1hr 10min
No. 8 S Ch Light	+2hrs 30min
Point Cook	+3hrs 10min
Port Albert Pier	+1hr 30min
Port Fairy	-51min
Port Phillip Hds	0
Rabbit Island	+10min
Port Welshpool Pier	+1hr 21min
Portland	-50min
Portlarington	+3hrs 15min
Portsea	+1hr 20min
Queenscliff	+35min
Refuge Cove	+ 36min
Rhyll	+1hr
Rip Bank	-15min
Rosebud	+3hrs 20min
Rye	+3hrs
Sandringham	+3hrs 20min
Seal Rock	0
Seaspray	-3hrs 11min
Shallow Inlet	+13min
Singapore Deep	- 25min
Sorrento	+2hrs 15min
S. Ch Pile Light	+3hrs 10min
St Kilda	+3hrs 20min
St Leonards	+3hrs 15min
Stony Point	+1hr
Swan Island Dock	+2hrs
Tarwin River	+3hrs
Tooradin	+1hr 45min
Venus Bay	0
Warratah Bay	0
Warrnambool	-59min
Welshpool Pier	+1hr 30min
Werribee River	+3hrs 15min
W. Ch Pile Light	+3hrs 10min
Williamstown	+3hrs 25min
Woolami	0

Port Phillip Heads

Day	Date		Tide 1
Sun	1	○	12:17 AM (1.3) **H**
Mon	2		12:59 AM (1.4) **H**
Tue	3		1:37 AM (1.5) **H**
Wed	4		2:13 AM (1.5) **H**
Thu	5		2:48 AM (1.5) **H**
Fri	6		3:22 AM (1.5) **H**
Sat	7		3:57 AM (1.5) **H**
Sun	8		4:32 AM (1.5) **H**
Mon	9		5:09 AM (1.4) **H**
Tue	10		5:51 AM (1.3) **H**
Wed	11		12:00 AM (0.4) L
Thu	12		1:05 AM (0.5) L
Fri	13		2:22 AM (0.6) L
Sat	14		3:45 AM (0.6) L
Sun	15	●	5:03 AM (0.6) L
Mon	16		12:02 AM (1.5) **H**
Tue	17		12:57 AM (1.6) **H**
Wed	18		1:47 AM (1.7) **H**
Thu	19		2:34 AM (1.7) **H**
Fri	20		3:18 AM (1.7) **H**
Sat	21		4:01 AM (1.6) **H**
Sun	22		4:43 AM (1.6) **H**
Mon	23		5:24 AM (1.5) **H**
Tue	24		6:06 AM (1.4) **H**
Wed	25		12:17 AM (0.5) L
Thu	26		1:10 AM (0.6) L
Fri	27		2:13 AM (0.7) L
Sat	28		3:25 AM (0.7) L
Sun	29		4:39 AM (0.7) L
Mon	30	○	5:42 AM (0.7) L

During Daylight Savings Time add one hour to the times stated below.

NOVEMBER 2020

Tide 2		Tide 3		Tide 4	
6:19 AM	(0.6) L	12:00 PM	(1.3) **H**	6:26 PM	(0.3) L
7:02 AM	(0.6) L	12:39 PM	(1.3) **H**	7:02 PM	(0.2) L
7:41 AM	(0.5) L	1:14 PM	(1.3) **H**	7:36 PM	(0.2) L
8:17 AM	(0.5) L	1:47 PM	(1.3) **H**	8:09 PM	(0.2) L
8:52 AM	(0.5) L	2:18 PM	(1.3) **H**	8:41 PM	(0.1) L
9:25 AM	(0.5) L	2:50 PM	(1.3) **H**	9:14 PM	(0.1) L
9:59 AM	(0.6) L	3:22 PM	(1.3) **H**	9:48 PM	(0.2) L
10:33 AM	(0.6) L	3:58 PM	(1.2) **H**	10:25 PM	(0.2) L
11:11 AM	(0.6) L	4:41 PM	(1.2) **H**	11:08 PM	(0.3) L
11:56 AM	(0.6) L	5:37 PM	(1.2) **H**		
6:40 AM	(1.3) **H**	12:51 PM	(0.6) L	6:51 PM	(1.1) **H**
7:37 AM	(1.2) **H**	1:56 PM	(0.5) L	8:15 PM	(1.2) **H**
8:40 AM	(1.2) **H**	3:05 PM	(0.5) L	9:40 PM	(1.2) **H**
9:44 AM	(1.2) **H**	4:13 PM	(0.3) L	10:56 PM	(1.4) **H**
10:45 AM	(1.3) **H**	5:15 PM	(0.2) L		
6:08 AM	(0.6) L	11:42 AM	(1.3) **H**	6:11 PM	(0.1) L
7:04 AM	(0.5) L	12:34 PM	(1.4) **H**	7:02 PM	(0.0) L
7:53 AM	(0.5) L	1:23 PM	(1.4) **H**	7:50 PM	(0.0) L
8:39 AM	(0.5) L	2:10 PM	(1.4) **H**	8:36 PM	(0.0) L
9:23 AM	(0.5) L	2:56 PM	(1.4) **H**	9:20 PM	(0.1) L
10:06 AM	(0.5) L	3:42 PM	(1.4) **H**	10:03 PM	(0.1) L
10:50 AM	(0.5) L	4:30 PM	(1.3) **H**	10:46 PM	(0.3) L
11:35 AM	(0.5) L	5:20 PM	(1.2) **H**	11:30 PM	(0.4) L
12:22 PM	(0.5) L	6:17 PM	(1.2) **H**		
6:49 AM	(1.3) **H**	1:14 PM	(0.5) L	7:21 PM	(1.1) **H**
7:35 AM	(1.2) **H**	2:09 PM	(0.5) L	8:32 PM	(1.1) **H**
8:26 AM	(1.2) **H**	3:08 PM	(0.5) L	9:47 PM	(1.1) **H**
9:19 AM	(1.2) **H**	4:04 PM	(0.4) L	10:54 PM	(1.2) **H**
10:12 AM	(1.2) **H**	4:55 PM	(0.4) L	11:47 PM	(1.3) **H**
11:02 AM	(1.2) **H**	5:40 PM	(0.3) L		

Port Phillip Heads

POPULAR TIDE ADJUSTMENTS

Location	Adjustment
Altona	+3hrs 25min
Anderson Inlet	+10min
Anglesea	-30min
Apollo Bay	-25min
Barwon Heads	+15min
Black Rock	+3hrs 2min
Cape Otway	-30min
Cape Patterson	0
Cape Schanack	0
Carrum	+3hrs 15min
Corinella	+1hr 8min
Cnr Inlet Ent.	+25min
Cowes	+1hr 15min
Dromana	+3hrs 20min
Flinders	+48min
Frankston	+3hrs 20min
Geelong	+3hrs 30min
Golden Beach	-1hr 30min
Gunnamatta	-25min
Hastings	+1hr 15min
Hovell Pile	+3hrs 20min
Inverloch	+20min
Kilcunda	+10min
K. Is (Franklin)	-40min
K. Is(Grassy)	-10min
K. Is(Surprise Bay)	-40min
Lake Tyers	-2hrs 57min
Lakes Entrance	-2hrs 50min
Lang Lang	+1hr 55min
Lochspot	-1hr 30min
Lorne	-20min
Mahers Landing	+1hr 30min
Mallacoota Inlet	-2hrs 38min
Maribynong Riv'	+3hrs 15min
McLoughins	+2hrs 25min
McLoughlins Bch	-1hr
Melbourne	+3hrs 30min
Mordialloc	+3hrs 5min
Mornington	+3hrs 20min
New Haven	+1hr 25min
No. 1 W Ch (Annulus)	+50min
No. 2 S Ch Light	+1hr 10min
No. 8 S Ch Light	+2hrs 30min
Point Cook	+3hrs 10min
Port Albert Pier	+1hr 30min
Port Fairy	-51min
Port Phillip Hds	0
Rabbit Island	+10min
Port Welshpool Pier	+1hr 21min
Portland	-50min
Portlarington	+3hrs 15min
Portsea	+1hr 20min
Queenscliff	+35min
Refuge Cove	+ 36min
Rhyll	+1hr
Rip Bank	-15min
Rosebud	+3hrs 20min
Rye	+3hrs
Sandringham	+3hrs 20min
Seal Rock	0
Seaspray	-3hrs 11min
Shallow Inlet	+13min
Singapore Deep	- 25min
Sorrento	+2hrs 15min
S. Ch Pile Light	+3hrs 10min
St Kilda	+3hrs 20min
St Leonards	+3hrs 15min
Stony Point	+1hr
Swan Island Dock	+2hrs
Tarwin River	+3hrs
Tooradin	+1hr 45min
Venus Bay	0
Warratah Bay	0
Warrnambool	-59min
Welshpool Pier	+1hr 30min
Werribee River	+3hrs 15min
W. Ch Pile Light	+3hrs 10min
Williamstown	+3hrs 25min
Woolami	0

Day	Date		Tide 1
Tue	1		12:32 AM (1.4) **H**
Wed	2		1:12 AM (1.5) **H**
Thu	3		1:50 AM (1.5) **H**
Fri	4		2:27 AM (1.5) **H**
Sat	5		3:02 AM (1.5) **H**
Sun	6		3:37 AM (1.5) **H**
Mon	7		4:11 AM (1.5) **H**
Tue	8		4:47 AM (1.4) **H**
Wed	9		5:26 AM (1.4) **H**
Thu	10		6:10 AM (1.3) **H**
Fri	11		12:45 AM (0.5) L
Sat	12		1:54 AM (0.6) L
Sun	13		3:12 AM (0.7) L
Mon	14		4:33 AM (0.7) L
Tue	15	●	5:46 AM (0.7) L
Wed	16		12:44 AM (1.6) **H**
Thu	17		1:35 AM (1.6) **H**
Fri	18		2:22 AM (1.7) **H**
Sat	19		3:05 AM (1.6) **H**
Sun	20		3:45 AM (1.6) **H**
Mon	21		4:23 AM (1.5) **H**
Tue	22		4:59 AM (1.5) **H**
Wed	23		5:34 AM (1.4) **H**
Thu	24		6:08 AM (1.3) **H**
Fri	25		12:31 AM (0.6) L
Sat	26		1:21 AM (0.7) L
Sun	27		2:22 AM (0.8) L
Mon	28		3:34 AM (0.8) L
Tue	29		4:50 AM (0.8) L
Wed	30	○	12:00 AM (1.3) **H**
Thu	31		12:47 AM (1.4) **H**

During Daylight Savings Time add one hour to the times stated below.

DECEMBER 2020

Tide 2		Tide 3		Tide 4	
6:33 AM	(0.7) L	11:47 AM	(1.2) **H**	6:21 PM	(0.2) L
7:17 AM	(0.6) L	12:30 PM	(1.2) **H**	6:59 PM	(0.2) L
7:56 AM	(0.6) L	1:09 PM	(1.2) **H**	7:37 PM	(0.1) L
8:33 AM	(0.6) L	1:47 PM	(1.2) **H**	8:13 PM	(0.1) L
9:08 AM	(0.6) L	2:25 PM	(1.2) **H**	8:50 PM	(0.1) L
9:42 AM	(0.5) L	3:05 PM	(1.2) **H**	9:28 PM	(0.1) L
10:18 AM	(0.5) L	3:49 PM	(1.2) **H**	10:09 PM	(0.2) L
10:57 AM	(0.5) L	4:39 PM	(1.2) **H**	10:54 PM	(0.3) L
11:41 AM	(0.5) L	5:38 PM	(1.2) **H**	11:45 PM	(0.4) L
12:32 PM	(0.4) L	6:47 PM	(1.2) **H**		
7:00 AM	(1.3) **H**	1:31 PM	(0.4) L	8:03 PM	(1.2) **H**
7:57 AM	(1.3) **H**	2:35 PM	(0.3) L	9:22 PM	(1.3) **H**
8:59 AM	(1.3) **H**	3:41 PM	(0.2) L	10:39 PM	(1.4) **H**
10:03 AM	(1.3) **H**	4:46 PM	(0.2) L	11:47 PM	(1.5) **H**
11:06 AM	(1.3) **H**	5:47 PM	(0.1) L		
6:47 AM	(0.6) L	12:06 PM	(1.3) **H**	6:43 PM	(0.0) L
7:40 AM	(0.6) L	1:02 PM	(1.4) **H**	7:34 PM	(0.0) L
8:28 AM	(0.5) L	1:55 PM	(1.4) **H**	8:21 PM	(0.0) L
9:12 AM	(0.5) L	2:46 PM	(1.4) **H**	9:06 PM	(0.1) L
9:55 AM	(0.4) L	3:34 PM	(1.3) **H**	9:48 PM	(0.2) L
10:36 AM	(0.4) L	4:22 PM	(1.3) **H**	10:28 PM	(0.3) L
11:17 AM	(0.4) L	5:10 PM	(1.2) **H**	11:07 PM	(0.4) L
11:57 AM	(0.4) L	6:00 PM	(1.2) **H**	11:47 PM	(0.5) L
12:39 PM	(0.4) L	6:53 PM	(1.1) **H**		
6:45 AM	(1.3) **H**	1:24 PM	(0.4) L	7:52 PM	(1.1) **H**
7:25 AM	(1.2) **H**	2:12 PM	(0.4) L	8:57 PM	(1.1) **H**
8:11 AM	(1.2) **H**	3:03 PM	(0.4) L	10:04 PM	(1.2) **H**
9:04 AM	(1.1) **H**	3:57 PM	(0.3) L	11:07 PM	(1.2) **H**
9:59 AM	(1.1) **H**	4:50 PM	(0.3) L		
5:57 AM	(0.8) L	10:55 AM	(1.1) **H**	5:40 PM	(0.2) L
6:51 AM	(0.7) L	11:48 AM	(1.1) **H**	6:27 PM	(0.2) L

Apogee moon phase on Saturday 17th
Perigee moon phase on Friday 2nd & Saturday 31st
● New moon on Thursday 1st & Friday 30th
First quarter moon on Thursday 8th
○ Full moon on Thursday 15th
Last quarter moon phase on Saturday 24th

Melbourne, VIC: Rise: 07:00am Set: 05:40pm

(Note: These sun rise/set times are averages for the month)

DAY	MINOR BITE	MAJOR BITE	MINOR BITE	MAJOR BITE	SALT WATER RATING	FRESH WATER RATING
THUR 1	6:23 AM	11:27 AM	4:35 PM	11:56 PM	● 8	8
FRI 2	7:12 AM	12:27 PM	5:49 PM		8	6
SAT 3	7:54 AM	1:25 PM	7:03 PM	12:56 AM	7	6
SUN 4	8:32 AM	2:19 PM	8:15 PM	1:52 AM	6	7
MON 5	9:07 AM	3:12 PM	9:26 PM	2:45 AM	5	5
TUE 6	9:40 AM	4:02 PM	10:34 PM	3:37 AM	4	6
WED 7	10:13 AM	4:52 PM	11:41 PM	4:27 AM	3	5
THUR 8	10:47 AM	5:43 PM		5:17 AM	4	6
FRI 9	11:24 AM	6:33 PM	12:46 AM	6:08 AM	5	6
SAT 10	12:04 PM	7:24 PM	1:49 AM	6:58 AM	4	5
SUN 11	12:49 PM	8:16 PM	2:49 AM	7:49 AM	3	5

AUGUST 2019

POPULAR LOCATION ADJUSTMENTS (See full list on page 7)

DAY	MINOR BITE	MAJOR BITE	MINOR BITE	MAJOR BITE	SALT WATER RATING	FRESH WATER RATING
MON 12	1:38 PM	9:07 PM	3:45 AM	8:41 AM	6	6
TUE 13	2:31 PM	9:58 PM	4:36 AM	9:32 AM	5	7
WED 14	3:26 PM	10:46 PM	5:21 AM	10:22 AM	3	8
THUR 15	4:23 PM	11:33 PM	6:00 AM	11:09 AM	○ 5	7
FRI 16	5:20 PM		6:35 AM	11:54 AM	5	7
SAT 17	6:17 PM	12:17 AM	7:06 AM	12:38 PM	7	6
SUN 18	7:13 PM	1:00 AM	7:35 AM	1:20 PM	7	6
MON 19	8:09 PM	1:41 AM	8:02 AM	2:01 PM	5	5
TUE 20	9:06 PM	2:22 AM	8:28 AM	2:43 PM	4	4
WED 21	10:03 PM	3:04 AM	8:55 AM	3:25 PM	3	6
THUR 22	11:02 PM	3:47 AM	9:24 AM	4:09 PM	4	4
FRI 23		4:32 AM	9:55 AM	4:56 PM	5	5
SAT 24	12:03 AM	5:20 AM	10:32 AM	5:45 PM	5	5
SUN 25	1:06 AM	6:12 AM	11:14 AM	6:39 PM	6	6
MON 26	2:09 AM	7:07 AM	12:04 PM	7:36 PM	7	8
TUE 27	3:10 AM	8:06 AM	1:03 PM	8:36 PM	5	8
WED 28	4:07 AM	9:07 AM	2:09 PM	9:37 PM	6	7
THUR 29	4:59 AM	10:08 AM	3:22 PM	10:37 PM	8	8
FRI 30	5:45 AM	11:07 AM	4:37 PM	11:35 PM	● 8	8
SAT 31	6:25 AM	12:04 PM	5:52 PM		8	6

Apogee moon phase on Friday 13th
Perigee moon phase on Saturday 28th
● New moon on Sunday 29th
First quarter moon on Friday 6th
○ Full moon on Saturday 14th
Last quarter moon phase on Sunday 22nd

Melbourne, VIC: Rise: 06:20am Set: 06:10pm
(Note: These sun rise/set times are averages for the month)

DAY	MINOR BITE	MAJOR BITE	MINOR BITE	MAJOR BITE	SALT WATER RATING	FRESH WATER RATING
SUN 1	7:02 AM	12:59 PM	7:06 PM	12:31 AM	7	6
MON 2	7:37 AM	1:52 PM	8:18 PM	1:25 AM	6	7
TUE 3	8:11 AM	2:44 PM	9:28 PM	2:17 AM	5	5
WED 4	8:45 AM	3:36 PM	10:36 PM	3:09 AM	4	6
THUR 5	9:22 AM	4:28 PM	11:41 PM	4:01 AM	3	5
FRI 6	10:02 AM	5:20 PM		4:54 AM	4	6
SAT 7	10:46 AM	6:12 PM	12:44 AM	5:46 AM	5	6
SUN 8	11:34 AM	7:04 PM	1:41 AM	6:38 AM	4	5
MON 9	12:26 PM	7:55 PM	2:34 AM	7:29 AM	3	5
TUE 10	1:21 PM	8:43 PM	3:20 AM	8:18 AM	3	5
WED 11	2:17 PM	9:30 PM	4:01 AM	9:06 AM	6	6

SEPTEMBER 2019

POPULAR LOCATION ADJUSTMENTS (See full list on page 7)

DAY	MINOR BITE	MAJOR BITE	MINOR BITE	MAJOR BITE	SALT WATER RATING	FRESH WATER RATING
THUR 12	3:14 PM	10:15 PM	4:37 AM	9:52 AM	5	7
FRI 13	4:11 PM	10:58 PM	5:09 AM	10:36 AM	3	8
SAT 14	5:08 PM	11:40 PM	5:38 AM	11:18 AM	○ 5	7
SUN 15	6:04 PM		6:05 AM	12:01 PM	7	6
MON 16	7:00 PM	12:22 AM	6:32 AM	12:42 PM	7	6
TUE 17	7:58 PM	1:03 AM	6:58 AM	1:24 PM	5	5
WED 18	8:56 PM	1:45 AM	7:26 AM	2:07 PM	5	5
THUR 19	9:56 PM	2:29 AM	7:56 AM	2:52 PM	4	4
FRI 20	10:57 PM	3:15 AM	8:30 AM	3:39 PM	3	6
SAT 21	11:58 PM	4:05 AM	9:09 AM	4:31 PM	4	4
SUN 22		4:58 AM	9:55 AM	5:25 PM	5	5
MON 23	12:58 AM	5:53 AM	10:48 AM	6:22 PM	6	6
TUE 24	1:55 AM	6:51 AM	11:49 AM	7:20 PM	7	7
WED 25	2:48 AM	7:50 AM	12:57 PM	8:19 PM	7	8
THUR 26	3:35 AM	8:49 AM	2:10 PM	9:17 PM	5	8
FRI 27	4:17 AM	9:46 AM	3:24 PM	10:14 PM	6	7
SAT 28	4:55 AM	10:42 AM	4:38 PM	11:08 PM	8	8
SUN 29	5:30 AM	11:36 AM	5:52 PM		● 8	8
MON 30	6:05 AM	12:30 PM	7:05 PM	12:03 AM	8	6

Apogee moon phase on Friday 11th
Perigee moon phase on Saturday 26th
● New moon on Monday 28th
First quarter moon on Sunday 6th
○ Full moon on Monday 14th
Last quarter moon phase on Monday 21st

Melbourne, VIC: Rise: 06:30am Set: 07:30pm

Note: Daylight Savings start (clocks turn forward 1 hour) on Sunday, October 6th at 2:00 AM.
Subtract 1 hour to rise/set time for days before October 6th. These sun rise/set times are averages for the month.

DAY	MINOR BITE	MAJOR BITE	MINOR BITE	MAJOR BITE	SALT WATER RATING	FRESH WATER RATING
TUE 1	6:39 AM	1:23 PM	8:17 PM	12:56 AM	7	6
WED 2	7:16 AM	2:17 PM	9:26 PM	1:49 AM	6	7
THUR 3	7:56 AM	3:11 PM	10:32 PM	2:44 AM	5	5
FRI 4	8:40 AM	4:05 PM	11:34 PM	3:38 AM	4	6
SAT 5	9:28 AM	4:58 PM		4:31 AM	3	5
SUN 6	10:19 AM	5:50 PM	12:29 AM	5:24 AM	4	6
MON 7	11:14 AM	6:40 PM	1:19 AM	6:15 AM	5	6
TUE 8	12:10 PM	7:28 PM	2:01 AM	7:03 AM	4	5
WED 9	1:07 PM	8:13 PM	2:39 AM	7:50 AM	3	5
THUR 10	2:04 PM	8:57 PM	3:12 AM	8:35 AM	6	6
FRI 11	3:01 PM	9:39 PM	3:42 AM	9:18 AM	5	7

OCTOBER 2019

POPULAR LOCATION ADJUSTMENTS (See full list on page 7)

DAY	MINOR BITE	MAJOR BITE	MINOR BITE	MAJOR BITE	SALT WATER RATING	FRESH WATER RATING
SAT 12	3:58 PM	10:20 PM	4:09 AM	9:59 AM	5	7
SUN 13	4:54 PM	11:02 PM	4:35 AM	10:41 AM	3	8
MON 14	5:52 PM	11:44 PM	5:02 AM	11:22 AM	○ 5	7
TUE 15	6:50 PM		5:29 AM	12:05 PM	7	6
WED 16	7:50 PM	12:28 AM	5:58 AM	12:50 PM	7	6
THUR 17	8:51 PM	1:13 AM	6:31 AM	1:37 PM	5	5
FRI 18	9:52 PM	2:02 AM	7:08 AM	2:27 PM	4	4
SAT 19	10:53 PM	2:53 AM	7:51 AM	3:20 PM	3	6
SUN 20	11:50 PM	3:47 AM	8:41 AM	4:15 PM	4	4
MON 21		4:44 AM	9:39 AM	5:12 PM	5	5
TUE 22	12:42 AM	5:41 AM	10:42 AM	6:08 PM	6	6
WED 23	1:30 AM	6:37 AM	11:51 AM	7:04 PM	7	7
THUR 24	2:12 AM	7:33 AM	1:02 PM	8:00 PM	7	8
FRI 25	2:49 AM	8:28 AM	2:14 PM	8:54 PM	5	8
SAT 26	3:25 AM	9:21 AM	3:26 PM	9:47 PM	6	7
SUN 27	3:59 AM	10:14 AM	4:39 PM	10:40 PM	8	8
MON 28	4:33 AM	11:07 AM	5:51 PM	11:33 PM	● 8	8
TUE 29	5:08 AM	12:01 PM	7:03 PM		8	6
WED 30	5:47 AM	12:56 PM	8:13 PM	12:28 AM	7	6
THUR 31	6:29 AM	1:51 PM	9:19 PM	1:23 AM	6	7

Apogee moon phase on Thursday 7th
Perigee moon phase on Saturday 23rd
● New moon on Wednesday 27th
First quarter moon on Monday 4th
○ Full moon on Tuesday 12th
Last quarter moon phase on Wednesday 20th

Melbourne, VIC: Rise: 06:00am Set: 08:10pm

(Note: These sun rise/set times are averages for the month)

DAY	MINOR BITE	MAJOR BITE	MINOR BITE	MAJOR BITE	SALT WATER RATING	FRESH WATER RATING
FRI 1	7:17 AM	2:47 PM	10:19 PM	2:19 AM	5	5
SAT 2	8:08 AM	3:41 PM	11:13 PM	3:14 AM	4	6
SUN 3	9:03 AM	4:33 PM	11:59 PM	4:06 AM	3	5
MON 4	10:00 AM	5:23 PM		4:58 AM	4	6
TUE 5	10:58 AM	6:09 PM	12:39 AM	5:46 AM	5	6
WED 6	11:55 AM	6:54 PM	1:14 AM	6:31 AM	5	6
THUR 7	12:52 PM	7:36 PM	1:44 AM	7:15 AM	4	5
FRI 8	1:49 PM	8:18 PM	2:12 AM	7:57 AM	3	5
SAT 9	2:46 PM	8:59 PM	2:39 AM	8:38 AM	6	6
SUN 10	3:43 PM	9:41 PM	3:05 AM	9:20 AM	5	7
MON 11	4:41 PM	10:24 PM	3:32 AM	10:02 AM	3	8

NOVEMBER 2019

POPULAR LOCATION ADJUSTMENTS (See full list on page 7)

DAY	MINOR BITE	MAJOR BITE	MINOR BITE	MAJOR BITE	SALT WATER RATING	FRESH WATER RATING
TUE 12	5:42 PM	11:10 PM	4:00 AM	10:46 AM	○ 5	7
WED 13	6:43 PM	11:58 PM	4:32 AM	11:33 AM	5	7
THUR 14	7:46 PM		5:07 AM	12:23 PM	7	6
FRI 15	8:48 PM	12:49 AM	5:49 AM	1:16 PM	7	6
SAT 16	9:47 PM	1:43 AM	6:37 AM	2:11 PM	5	5
SUN 17	10:41 PM	2:39 AM	7:33 AM	3:07 PM	4	4
MON 18	11:29 PM	3:36 AM	8:34 AM	4:04 PM	3	6
TUE 19		4:33 AM	9:41 AM	5:00 PM	4	4
WED 20	12:12 AM	5:27 AM	10:49 AM	5:53 PM	5	5
THUR 21	12:50 AM	6:21 AM	11:59 AM	6:46 PM	6	6
FRI 22	1:24 AM	7:12 AM	1:09 PM	7:37 PM	7	7
SAT 23	1:57 AM	8:03 AM	2:19 PM	8:28 PM	7	8
SUN 24	2:29 AM	8:54 AM	3:29 PM	9:20 PM	5	8
MON 25	3:03 AM	9:47 AM	4:40 PM	10:13 PM	6	7
TUE 26	3:39 AM	10:40 AM	5:50 PM	11:07 PM	8	8
WED 27	4:19 AM	11:35 AM	6:58 PM		● 8	8
THUR 28	5:04 AM	12:31 PM	8:03 PM	12:03 AM	8	6
FRI 29	5:54 AM	1:27 PM	9:01 PM	12:59 AM	7	6
SAT 30	6:49 AM	2:22 PM	9:52 PM	1:54 AM	6	7

Apogee moon phase on Thursday 5th
Perigee moon phase on Thursday 19th
● New moon on Thursday 26th
First quarter moon on Wednesday 4th
○ Full moon on Thursday 12th
Last quarter moon phase on Thursday 19th

Melbourne, VIC: Rise: 05:50am Set: 08:30pm

(Note: These sun rise/set times are averages for the month)

DAY	MINOR BITE	MAJOR BITE	MINOR BITE	MAJOR BITE	SALT WATER RATING	FRESH WATER RATING
SUN 1	7:46 AM	3:13 PM	10:35 PM	2:47 AM	5	5
MON 2	8:45 AM	4:02 PM	11:13 PM	3:37 AM	4	6
TUE 3	9:44 AM	4:48 PM	11:45 PM	4:25 AM	3	5
WED 4	10:41 AM	5:32 PM		5:10 AM	4	6
THUR 5	11:38 AM	6:14 PM	12:14 AM	5:53 AM	5	6
FRI 6	12:35 PM	6:55 PM	12:41 AM	6:34 AM	4	5
SAT 7	1:31 PM	7:36 PM	1:07 AM	7:15 AM	4	5
SUN 8	2:29 PM	8:18 PM	1:33 AM	7:57 AM	3	5
MON 9	3:28 PM	9:03 PM	2:00 AM	8:40 AM	6	6
TUE 10	4:30 PM	9:50 PM	2:30 AM	9:26 AM	5	7
WED 11	5:33 PM	10:41 PM	3:04 AM	10:15 AM	3	8

DECEMBER 2019

POPULAR LOCATION ADJUSTMENTS (See full list on page 7)

DAY	MINOR BITE	MAJOR BITE	MINOR BITE	MAJOR BITE	SALT WATER RATING	FRESH WATER RATING
THUR 12	6:37 PM	11:35 PM	3:44 AM	11:07 AM	○ 5	7
FRI 13	7:38 PM		4:30 AM	12:03 PM	7	6
SAT 14	8:36 PM	12:32 AM	5:24 AM	1:01 PM	7	6
SUN 15	9:28 PM	1:30 AM	6:26 AM	1:58 PM	5	5
MON 16	10:13 PM	2:28 AM	7:32 AM	2:56 PM	4	4
TUE 17	10:52 PM	3:24 AM	8:41 AM	3:50 PM	3	6
WED 18	11:27 PM	4:18 AM	9:51 AM	4:43 PM	4	4
THUR 19	12:00 AM	5:09 AM	11:00 AM	5:34 PM	5	5
FRI 20		6:00 AM	12:08 PM	6:24 PM	6	6
SAT 21	12:31 AM	6:49 AM	1:17 PM	7:14 PM	7	7
SUN 22	1:03 AM	7:39 AM	2:25 PM	8:04 PM	7	8
MON 23	1:37 AM	8:30 AM	3:33 PM	8:56 PM	5	8
TUE 24	2:14 AM	9:23 AM	4:41 PM	9:50 PM	6	7
WED 25	2:56 AM	10:18 AM	5:46 PM	10:45 PM	8	8
THUR 26	3:43 AM	11:14 AM	6:47 PM	11:41 PM	● 8	8
FRI 27	4:35 AM	12:09 PM	7:41 PM		8	6
SAT 28	5:32 AM	1:02 PM	8:29 PM	12:35 AM	7	6
SUN 29	6:31 AM	1:53 PM	9:09 PM	1:27 AM	6	7
MON 30	7:30 AM	2:41 PM	9:44 PM	2:16 AM	6	7
TUE 31	8:29 AM	3:26 PM	10:15 PM	3:03 AM	5	5

Apogee moon phase on Thursday 2nd
Perigee moon phase on Tuesday 14th
● New moon on Saturday 25th
First quarter moon on Friday 3rd
○ Full moon on Saturday 11th
Last quarter moon phase on Friday 17th

Melbourne, VIC: Rise: 06:10am Set: 08:40pm

(Note: These sun rise/set times are averages for the month)

DAY	MINOR BITE	MAJOR BITE	MINOR BITE	MAJOR BITE	SALT WATER RATING	FRESH WATER RATING
WED 1	9:26 AM	4:09 PM	10:43 PM	3:47 AM	4	6
THUR 2	10:23 AM	4:50 PM	11:09 PM	4:29 AM	3	5
FRI 3	11:19 AM	5:31 PM	11:34 PM	5:10 AM	4	6
SAT 4	12:16 PM	6:12 PM		5:51 AM	5	6
SUN 5	1:14 PM	6:55 PM	12:00 AM	6:33 AM	4	5
MON 6	2:13 PM	7:40 PM	12:29 AM	7:17 AM	3	5
TUE 7	3:15 PM	8:29 PM	1:00 AM	8:04 AM	6	6
WED 8	4:19 PM	9:21 PM	1:37 AM	8:54 AM	6	6
THUR 9	5:22 PM	10:17 PM	2:20 AM	9:48 AM	5	7
FRI 10	6:23 PM	11:16 PM	3:11 AM	10:46 AM	3	8
SAT 11	7:19 PM		4:10 AM	11:46 AM	○ 5	7

JANUARY 2020

POPULAR LOCATION ADJUSTMENTS (See full list on page 7)

DAY	MINOR BITE	MAJOR BITE	MINOR BITE	MAJOR BITE	SALT WATER RATING	FRESH WATER RATING
SUN 12	8:08 PM	12:16 AM	5:16 AM	12:45 PM	7	6
MON 13	8:51 PM	1:15 AM	6:27 AM	1:43 PM	7	6
TUE 14	9:28 PM	2:11 AM	7:39 AM	2:37 PM	5	5
WED 15	10:02 PM	3:05 AM	8:50 AM	3:31 PM	4	4
THUR 16	10:34 PM	3:57 AM	10:00 AM	4:22 PM	3	6
FRI 17	11:06 PM	4:47 AM	11:09 AM	5:11 PM	5	5
SAT 18	11:39 PM	5:37 AM	12:17 PM	6:02 PM	6	6
SUN 19		6:27 AM	1:25 PM	6:52 PM	6	6
MON 20	12:14 AM	7:18 AM	2:31 PM	7:44 PM	7	7
TUE 21	12:53 AM	8:11 AM	3:36 PM	8:37 PM	7	8
WED 22	1:37 AM	9:05 AM	4:37 PM	9:32 PM	5	8
THUR 23	2:27 AM	10:00 AM	5:33 PM	10:26 PM	6	7
FRI 24	3:21 AM	10:53 AM	6:23 PM	11:18 PM	8	8
SAT 25	4:19 AM	11:45 AM	7:05 PM		● 8	8
SUN 26	5:18 AM	12:34 PM	7:42 PM	12:09 AM	8	6
MON 27	6:17 AM	1:20 PM	8:15 PM	12:57 AM	7	6
TUE 28	7:16 AM	2:04 PM	8:44 PM	1:42 AM	6	7
WED 29	8:13 AM	2:45 PM	9:10 PM	2:24 AM	5	5
THUR 30	9:09 AM	3:26 PM	9:36 PM	3:05 AM	5	5
FRI 31	10:05 AM	4:07 PM	10:01 PM	3:46 AM	4	60

Apogee moon phase on Wednesday 26th
Perigee moon phase on Tuesday 11th
● New moon on Monday 24th
First quarter moon on Sunday 2nd
○ Full moon on Sunday 9th
Last quarter moon phase on Sunday 16th

Melbourne, VIC: Rise: 06:40am Set: 08:20pm

(Note: These sun rise/set times are averages for the month)

DAY	MINOR BITE	MAJOR BITE	MINOR BITE	MAJOR BITE	SALT WATER RATING	FRESH WATER RATING
SAT 1	11:02 AM	4:48 PM	10:28 PM	4:27 AM	3	5
SUN 2	12:00 PM	5:32 PM	10:57 PM	5:10 AM	4	6
MON 3	12:59 PM	6:18 PM	11:31 PM	5:55 AM	5	6
TUE 4	2:01 PM	7:07 PM		6:42 AM	4	5
WED 5	3:03 PM	8:01 PM	12:09 AM	7:33 AM	3	5
THUR 6	4:04 PM	8:58 PM	12:56 AM	8:29 AM	6	6
FRI 7	5:03 PM	9:57 PM	1:50 AM	9:27 AM	5	7
SAT 8	5:56 PM	10:57 PM	2:53 AM	10:26 AM	3	8
SUN 9	6:42 PM	11:56 PM	4:03 AM	11:26 AM	○ 5	7
MON 10	7:23 PM		5:16 AM	12:24 PM	7	6

POPULAR LOCATION ADJUSTMENTS (See full list on page 7)

DAY	MINOR BITE	MAJOR BITE	MINOR BITE	MAJOR BITE	SALT WATER RATING	FRESH WATER RATING
TUE 11	8:00 PM	12:53 AM	6:31 AM	1:20 PM	7	6
WED 12	8:34 PM	1:48 AM	7:44 AM	2:13 PM	5	5
THUR 13	9:07 PM	2:40 AM	8:56 AM	3:05 PM	4	4
FRI 14	9:40 PM	3:32 AM	10:07 AM	3:57 PM	3	6
SAT 15	10:15 PM	4:23 AM	11:16 AM	4:48 PM	4	4
SUN 16	10:53 PM	5:15 AM	12:24 PM	5:41 PM	5	5
MON 17	11:35 PM	6:08 AM	1:30 PM	6:34 PM	6	6
TUE 18		7:01 AM	2:32 PM	7:27 PM	7	7
WED 19	12:23 AM	7:55 AM	3:29 PM	8:21 PM	7	8
THUR 20	1:15 AM	8:48 AM	4:20 PM	9:14 PM	5	8
FRI 21	2:11 AM	9:40 AM	5:04 PM	10:04 PM	6	7
SAT 22	3:10 AM	10:29 AM	5:42 PM	10:52 PM	8	8
SUN 23	4:09 AM	11:16 AM	6:16 PM	11:37 PM	8	8
MON 24	5:07 AM	12:00 PM	6:45 PM		● 8	8
TUE 25	6:05 AM	12:43 PM	7:13 PM	12:21 AM	8	6
WED 26	7:01 AM	1:24 PM	7:38 PM	1:03 AM	7	6
THUR 27	7:57 AM	2:04 PM	8:04 PM	1:44 AM	6	7
FRI 28	8:54 AM	2:45 PM	8:30 PM	2:24 AM	5	5
SAT 29	9:50 AM	3:27 PM	8:57 PM	3:06 AM	4	6

Apogee moon phase on Wednesday 25th
Perigee moon phase on Tuesday 10th
● New moon on Tuesday 24th
First quarter moon on Tuesday 3rd
○ Full moon on Tuesday 10th
Last quarter moon phase on Monday 16th

Melbourne, VIC: Rise: 07:10am Set: 07:40pm

(Note: These sun rise/set times are averages for the month)

DAY	MINOR BITE	MAJOR BITE	MINOR BITE	MAJOR BITE	SALT WATER RATING	FRESH WATER RATING
SUN 1	10:49 AM	4:11 PM	9:28 PM	3:49 AM	3	5
MON 2	11:48 AM	4:58 PM	10:04 PM	4:34 AM	3	5
TUE 3	12:48 PM	5:48 PM	10:45 PM	5:23 AM	4	6
WED 4	1:49 PM	6:42 PM	11:34 PM	6:15 AM	5	6
THUR 5	2:47 PM	7:39 PM		7:10 AM	4	5
FRI 6	3:41 PM	8:38 PM	12:32 AM	8:08 AM	3	5
SAT 7	4:30 PM	9:36 PM	1:37 AM	9:07 AM	6	6
SUN 8	5:14 PM	10:34 PM	2:48 AM	10:05 AM	5	7
MON 9	5:53 PM	11:31 PM	4:03 AM	11:02 AM	3	8
TUE 10	6:28 PM		5:18 AM	11:58 AM	○ 5	7
WED 11	7:02 PM	12:26 AM	6:33 AM	12:52 PM	7	6

MARCH 2020

POPULAR LOCATION ADJUSTMENTS (See full list on page 7)

DAY	MINOR BITE	MAJOR BITE	MINOR BITE	MAJOR BITE	SALT WATER RATING	FRESH WATER RATING
THUR 12	7:36 PM	1:19 AM	7:47 AM	1:46 PM	7	6
FRI 13	8:12 PM	2:13 AM	9:00 AM	2:39 PM	4	4
SAT 14	8:50 PM	3:07 AM	10:11 AM	3:33 PM	3	6
SUN 15	9:32 PM	4:01 AM	11:20 AM	4:28 PM	4	4
MON 16	10:19 PM	4:56 AM	12:26 PM	5:23 PM	5	5
TUE 17	11:10 PM	5:51 AM	1:25 PM	6:18 PM	6	6
WED 18		6:45 AM	2:18 PM	7:11 PM	6	6
THUR 19	12:06 AM	7:37 AM	3:05 PM	8:02 PM	7	7
FRI 20	1:04 AM	8:27 AM	3:44 PM	8:50 PM	7	8
SAT 21	2:02 AM	9:14 AM	4:19 PM	9:36 PM	5	8
SUN 22	3:01 AM	9:59 AM	4:49 PM	10:19 PM	6	7
MON 23	3:58 AM	10:41 AM	5:16 PM	11:02 PM	8	8
TUE 24	4:55 AM	11:23 AM	5:42 PM	11:42 PM	● 8	8
WED 25	5:51 AM	12:03 PM	6:07 PM		8	6
THUR 26	6:48 AM	12:44 PM	6:33 PM	12:23 AM	8	6
FRI 27	7:44 AM	1:25 PM	7:00 PM	1:04 AM	7	6
SAT 28	8:42 AM	2:09 PM	7:29 PM	1:47 AM	6	7
SUN 29	9:41 AM	2:54 PM	8:02 PM	2:31 AM	5	5
MON 30	10:41 AM	3:43 PM	8:41 PM	3:18 AM	4	6
TUE 31	11:40 AM	4:34 PM	9:26 PM	4:08 AM	3	5

Apogee moon phase on Tuesday 21st
Perigee moon phase on Wednesday 8th
● New moon on Thursday 23rd
First quarter moon on Wednesday 1st
○ Full moon on Wednesday 8th
Last quarter moon phase on Wednesday 15th

Melbourne, VIC: Rise: 06:40am Set: 05:50pm

(Note: Daylight Savings ends (clocks turn backward 1 hour) on Sunday, 5th April at 3:00 AM. Add 1 hour to rise/set time for days before April 5th. These sun rise/set times are averages for the month.

DAY	MINOR BITE	MAJOR BITE	MINOR BITE	MAJOR BITE	SALT WATER RATING	FRESH WATER RATING
WED 1	12:38 PM	5:28 PM	10:19 PM	5:00 AM	4	6
THUR 2	1:32 PM	6:24 PM	11:19 PM	5:56 AM	5	6
FRI 3	2:21 PM	7:21 PM		6:52 AM	4	5
SAT 4	3:06 PM	8:18 PM	12:25 AM	7:49 AM	3	5
SUN 5	3:45 PM	9:13 PM	1:36 AM	8:45 AM	6	6
MON 6	4:21 PM	10:08 PM	2:50 AM	9:40 AM	5	7
TUE 7	4:56 PM	11:02 PM	4:04 AM	10:35 AM	3	8
WED 8	5:30 PM	11:56 PM	5:19 AM	11:28 AM	○ 5	7
THUR 9	6:04 PM		6:34 AM	12:23 PM	7	6
FRI 10	6:42 PM	12:51 AM	7:48 AM	1:18 PM	7	6
SAT 11	7:24 PM	1:47 AM	9:01 AM	2:15 PM	5	5

APRIL 2020

POPULAR LOCATION ADJUSTMENTS (See full list on page 7)

DAY	MINOR BITE	MAJOR BITE	MINOR BITE	MAJOR BITE	SALT WATER RATING	FRESH WATER RATING
SUN 12	8:10 PM	2:44 AM	10:11 AM	3:12 PM	4	4
MON 13	9:02 PM	3:41 AM	11:16 AM	4:09 PM	3	6
TUE 14	9:58 PM	4:38 AM	12:14 PM	5:04 PM	4	4
WED 15	10:56 PM	5:32 AM	1:03 PM	5:57 PM	5	5
THUR 16	11:55 PM	6:24 AM	1:45 PM	6:48 PM	6	6
FRI 17		7:12 AM	2:21 PM	7:34 PM	7	7
SAT 18	12:54 AM	7:57 AM	2:53 PM	8:18 PM	7	8
SUN 19	1:52 AM	8:41 AM	3:21 PM	9:01 PM	5	8
MON 20	2:49 AM	9:22 AM	3:47 PM	9:42 PM	5	8
TUE 21	3:45 AM	10:03 AM	4:12 PM	10:22 PM	6	7
WED 22	4:42 AM	10:43 AM	4:37 PM	11:03 PM	8	8
THUR 23	5:39 AM	11:24 AM	5:03 PM	11:45 PM	● 8	8
FRI 24	6:36 AM	12:07 PM	5:32 PM		8	6
SAT 25	7:35 AM	12:52 PM	6:03 PM	12:29 AM	7	6
SUN 26	8:35 AM	1:40 PM	6:40 PM	1:15 AM	6	7
MON 27	9:35 AM	2:30 PM	7:23 PM	2:05 AM	5	5
TUE 28	10:33 AM	3:23 PM	8:13 PM	2:56 AM	5	5
WED 29	11:28 AM	4:18 PM	9:09 PM	3:50 AM	4	6
THUR 30	12:18 PM	5:13 PM	10:12 PM	4:45 AM	3	5

Apogee moon phase on Monday 18th
Perigee moon phase on Wednesday 6th
● New moon on Saturday 23rd
First quarter moon on Friday 1st and Saturday 30th
○ Full moon on Thursday 7th
Last quarter moon phase on Friday 15th

Melbourne, VIC: Rise: 07:10am Set: 05:20pm

(Note: These sun rise/set times are averages for the month)

DAY	MINOR BITE	MAJOR BITE	MINOR BITE	MAJOR BITE	SALT WATER RATING	FRESH WATER RATING
FRI 1	1:03 PM	6:08 PM	11:19 PM	5:40 AM	4	6
SAT 2	1:42 PM	7:02 PM		6:34 AM	5	6
SUN 3	2:18 PM	7:55 PM	12:29 AM	7:28 AM	4	5
MON 4	2:52 PM	8:48 PM	1:41 AM	8:21 AM	3	5
TUE 5	3:24 PM	9:40 PM	2:53 AM	9:13 AM	6	6
WED 6	3:58 PM	10:34 PM	4:07 AM	10:07 AM	3	8
THUR 7	4:33 PM	11:29 PM	5:21 AM	11:01 AM	○ 5	7
FRI 8	5:13 PM		6:35 AM	11:57 AM	7	6
SAT 9	5:58 PM	12:26 AM	7:49 AM	12:55 PM	7	6
SUN 10	6:48 PM	1:25 AM	8:58 AM	1:54 PM	5	5
MON 11	7:44 PM	2:24 AM	10:01 AM	2:52 PM	4	4

MAY 2020

POPULAR LOCATION ADJUSTMENTS (See full list on page 7)

DAY	MINOR BITE	MAJOR BITE	MINOR BITE	MAJOR BITE	SALT WATER RATING	FRESH WATER RATING
TUE 12	8:43 PM	3:21 AM	10:56 AM	3:48 PM	3	6
WED 13	9:44 PM	4:16 AM	11:43 AM	4:41 PM	4	4
THUR 14	10:45 PM	5:06 AM	12:22 PM	5:30 PM	5	5
FRI 15	11:44 PM	5:54 AM	12:55 PM	6:15 PM	5	5
SAT 16		6:38 AM	1:24 PM	6:59 PM	6	6
SUN 17	12:41 AM	7:20 AM	1:51 PM	7:40 PM	7	7
MON 18	1:38 AM	8:01 AM	2:16 PM	8:21 PM	7	8
TUE 19	2:34 AM	8:41 AM	2:41 PM	9:01 PM	5	8
WED 20	3:31 AM	9:22 AM	3:06 PM	9:43 PM	6	7
THUR 21	4:29 AM	10:05 AM	3:34 PM	10:26 PM	8	8
FRI 22	5:28 AM	10:49 AM	4:05 PM	11:12 PM	8	8
SAT 23	6:28 AM	11:36 AM	4:40 PM		● 8	8
SUN 24	7:29 AM	12:26 PM	5:21 PM	12:01 AM	8	6
MON 25	8:28 AM	1:19 PM	6:09 PM	12:52 AM	7	6
TUE 26	9:25 AM	2:14 PM	7:04 PM	1:46 AM	6	7
WED 27	10:17 AM	3:09 PM	8:05 PM	2:41 AM	5	5
THUR 28	11:03 AM	4:04 PM	9:10 PM	3:36 AM	4	6
FRI 29	11:43 AM	4:58 PM	10:19 PM	4:30 AM	3	5
SAT 30	12:19 PM	5:49 PM	11:28 PM	5:23 AM	4	6
SUN 31	12:52 PM	6:40 PM		6:14 AM	5	6

Apogee moon phase on Monday 15th
Perigee moon phase on Wednesday 3rd and Tuesday 30th
● New moon on Sunday 21st
First quarter moon on Sunday 28th
○ Full moon on Saturday 6th
Last quarter moon phase on Saturday 13th

Melbourne, VIC: Rise: 07:30am Set: 05:00pm

(Note: These sun rise/set times are averages for the month)

DAY	MINOR BITE	MAJOR BITE	MINOR BITE	MAJOR BITE	SALT WATER RATING	FRESH WATER RATING
MON 1	1:24 PM	7:31 PM	12:37 AM	7:05 AM	4	5
TUE 2	1:55 PM	8:22 PM	1:48 AM	7:56 AM	3	5
WED 3	2:29 PM	9:15 PM	2:59 AM	8:48 AM	6	6
THUR 4	3:05 PM	10:10 PM	4:12 AM	9:42 AM	5	7
FRI 5	3:46 PM	11:07 PM	5:25 AM	10:38 AM	3	8
SAT 6	4:34 PM		6:36 AM	11:36 AM	○ 5	7
SUN 7	5:28 PM	12:06 AM	7:43 AM	12:35 PM	7	6
MON 8	6:26 PM	1:05 AM	8:43 AM	1:33 PM	7	6
TUE 9	7:28 PM	2:03 AM	9:35 AM	2:29 PM	5	5
WED 10	8:31 PM	2:56 AM	10:18 AM	3:20 PM	4	4
THUR 11	9:32 PM	3:46 AM	10:54 AM	4:09 PM	3	6

JUNE 2020

POPULAR LOCATION ADJUSTMENTS (See full list on page 7)

DAY	MINOR BITE	MAJOR BITE	MINOR BITE	MAJOR BITE	SALT WATER RATING	FRESH WATER RATING
FRI 12	10:31 PM	4:33 AM	11:26 AM	4:54 PM	4	4
SAT 13	11:29 PM	5:16 AM	11:54 AM	5:37 PM	5	5
SUN 14		5:58 AM	12:19 PM	6:18 PM	6	6
MON 15	12:25 AM	6:38 AM	12:44 PM	6:58 PM	7	7
TUE 16	1:21 AM	7:19 AM	1:09 PM	7:40 PM	7	7
WED 17	2:19 AM	8:01 AM	1:36 PM	8:22 PM	7	8
THUR 18	3:17 AM	8:44 AM	2:05 PM	9:07 PM	5	8
FRI 19	4:17 AM	9:30 AM	2:38 PM	9:55 PM	6	7
SAT 20	5:18 AM	10:20 AM	3:17 PM	10:45 PM	8	8
SUN 21	6:19 AM	11:12 AM	4:03 PM	11:39 PM	● 8	8
MON 22	7:18 AM	12:07 PM	4:56 PM		8	6
TUE 23	8:13 AM	1:04 PM	5:57 PM	12:35 AM	7	6
WED 24	9:01 AM	2:00 PM	7:02 PM	1:32 AM	6	7
THUR 25	9:44 AM	2:54 PM	8:10 PM	2:27 AM	5	5
FRI 26	10:22 AM	3:47 PM	9:20 PM	3:20 AM	4	6
SAT 27	10:55 AM	4:38 PM	10:29 PM	4:12 AM	3	5
SUN 28	11:27 AM	5:27 PM	11:37 PM	5:02 AM	4	6
MON 29	11:57 AM	6:17 PM		5:51 AM	5	6
TUE 30	12:29 PM	7:08 PM	12:47 AM	6:42 AM	4	5

Apogee moon phase on Monday 13th
Perigee moon phase on Saturday 25th
● New moon on Tuesday 21st
First quarter moon on Monday 27th
○ Full moon on Sunday 5th
Last quarter moon phase on Monday 13th

Melbourne, VIC: Rise: 07:30am Set: 05:20pm

(Note: These sun rise/set times are averages for the month)

DAY	MINOR BITE	MAJOR BITE	MINOR BITE	MAJOR BITE	SALT WATER RATING	FRESH WATER RATING
WED 1	1:03 PM	8:00 PM	1:57 AM	7:33 AM	3	5
THUR 2	1:41 PM	8:55 PM	3:07 AM	8:27 AM	6	6
FRI 3	2:24 PM	9:52 PM	4:18 AM	9:23 AM	5	7
SAT 4	3:14 PM	10:51 PM	5:26 AM	10:21 AM	3	8
SUN 5	4:11 PM	11:49 PM	6:29 AM	11:20 AM	○ 5	7
MON 6	5:12 PM		7:24 AM	12:16 PM	7	6
TUE 7	6:15 PM	12:44 AM	8:11 AM	1:10 PM	7	6
WED 8	7:17 PM	1:37 AM	8:51 AM	2:01 PM	5	5
THUR 9	8:18 PM	2:25 AM	9:25 AM	2:47 PM	5	5
FRI 10	9:17 PM	3:10 AM	9:54 AM	3:31 PM	4	4
SAT 11	10:14 PM	3:53 AM	10:21 AM	4:13 PM	3	6

JULY 2020

POPULAR LOCATION ADJUSTMENTS (See full list on page 7)

DAY	MINOR BITE	MAJOR BITE	MINOR BITE	MAJOR BITE	SALT WATER RATING	FRESH WATER RATING
SUN 12	11:11 PM	4:34 AM	10:46 AM	4:54 PM	4	4
MON 13		5:15 AM	11:11 AM	5:35 PM	5	5
TUE 14	12:08 AM	5:56 AM	11:37 AM	6:17 PM	6	6
WED 15	1:05 AM	6:38 AM	12:04 PM	7:00 PM	7	7
THUR 16	2:04 AM	7:23 AM	12:36 PM	7:46 PM	7	8
FRI 17	3:04 AM	8:10 AM	1:12 PM	8:36 PM	5	8
SAT 18	4:06 AM	9:02 AM	1:55 PM	9:29 PM	6	7
SUN 19	5:06 AM	9:56 AM	2:45 PM	10:24 PM	8	8
MON 20	6:03 AM	10:53 AM	3:44 PM	11:21 PM	8	8
TUE 21	6:55 AM	11:50 AM	4:49 PM		● 8	8
WED 22	7:41 AM	12:47 PM	5:58 PM	12:18 AM	8	6
THUR 23	8:21 AM	1:41 PM	7:09 PM	1:14 AM	7	6
FRI 24	8:57 AM	2:34 PM	8:19 PM	2:07 AM	6	7
SAT 25	9:29 AM	3:25 PM	9:29 PM	2:59 AM	5	5
SUN 26	10:00 AM	4:15 PM	10:39 PM	3:50 AM	3	5
MON 27	10:31 AM	5:05 PM	11:48 PM	4:40 AM	4	6
TUE 28	11:04 AM	5:56 PM		5:30 AM	5	6
WED 29	11:40 AM	6:49 PM	12:58 AM	6:22 AM	4	5
THUR 30	12:21 PM	7:44 PM	2:07 AM	7:16 AM	3	5
FRI 31	1:07 PM	8:41 PM	3:15 AM	8:12 AM	3	5

Apogee moon phase on Sunday 9th
Perigee moon phase on Friday 21st
● New moon on Wednesday 19th
First quarter moon on Wednesday 26th
○ Full moon on Tuesday 4th
Last quarter moon phase on Wednesday 12th

Melbourne, VIC: Rise: 07:00am Set: 05:40pm

(Note: These sun rise/set times are averages for the month)

DAY	MINOR BITE	MAJOR BITE	MINOR BITE	MAJOR BITE	SALT WATER RATING	FRESH WATER RATING
SAT 1	2:00 PM	9:38 PM	4:18 AM	9:09 AM	6	6
SUN 2	2:59 PM	10:34 PM	5:15 AM	10:05 AM	5	7
MON 3	4:01 PM	11:27 PM	6:05 AM	11:00 AM	3	8
TUE 4	5:03 PM		6:47 AM	11:52 AM	○ 5	7
WED 5	6:05 PM	12:17 AM	7:23 AM	12:40 PM	7	6
THUR 6	7:05 PM	1:04 AM	7:54 AM	1:26 PM	7	6
FRI 7	8:04 PM	1:48 AM	8:22 AM	2:09 PM	5	5
SAT 8	9:01 PM	2:30 AM	8:48 AM	2:50 PM	4	4
SUN 9	9:57 PM	3:10 AM	9:12 AM	3:30 PM	3	6
MON 10	10:54 PM	3:51 AM	9:38 AM	4:11 PM	4	4
TUE 11	11:52 PM	4:32 AM	10:04 AM	4:53 PM	4	4

AUGUST 2020

POPULAR LOCATION ADJUSTMENTS (See full list on page 7)

DAY	MINOR BITE	MAJOR BITE	MINOR BITE	MAJOR BITE	SALT WATER RATING	FRESH WATER RATING
WED 12		5:16 AM	10:33 AM	5:38 PM	5	5
THUR 13	12:51 AM	6:01 AM	11:07 AM	6:25 PM	6	6
FRI 14	1:51 AM	6:50 AM	11:46 AM	7:16 PM	7	7
SAT 15	2:51 AM	7:43 AM	12:33 PM	8:10 PM	7	8
SUN 16	3:50 AM	8:38 AM	1:27 PM	9:06 PM	5	8
MON 17	4:44 AM	9:35 AM	2:30 PM	10:03 PM	6	7
TUE 18	5:33 AM	10:33 AM	3:38 PM	11:00 PM	8	8
WED 19	6:16 AM	11:29 AM	4:50 PM	11:56 PM	● 8	8
THUR 20	6:54 AM	12:24 PM	6:03 PM		8	6
FRI 21	7:29 AM	1:17 PM	7:15 PM	12:50 AM	7	6
SAT 22	8:01 AM	2:09 PM	8:27 PM	1:42 AM	6	7
SUN 23	8:33 AM	3:00 PM	9:38 PM	2:34 AM	5	5
MON 24	9:05 AM	3:52 PM	10:50 PM	3:25 AM	4	6
TUE 25	9:41 AM	4:46 PM	12:00 AM	4:18 AM	3	5
WED 26	10:20 AM	5:40 PM		5:13 AM	4	6
THUR 27	11:05 AM	6:36 PM	1:08 AM	6:08 AM	5	6
FRI 28	11:55 AM	7:33 PM	2:12 AM	7:04 AM	4	5
SAT 29	12:51 PM	8:28 PM	3:11 AM	8:00 AM	3	5
SUN 30	1:51 PM	9:22 PM	4:02 AM	8:54 AM	6	6
MON 31	2:53 PM	10:12 PM	4:46 AM	9:46 AM	5	7

Apogee moon phase on Sunday 6th
Perigee moon phase on Friday 18th
● New moon on Thursday 17th
First quarter moon on Thursday 24th
○ Full moon on Wednesday 2nd
Last quarter moon phase on Thursday 10th

Melbourne, VIC: Rise: 06:20am Set: 06:10pm

(Note: These sun rise/set times are averages for the month)

DAY	MINOR BITE	MAJOR BITE	MINOR BITE	MAJOR BITE	SALT WATER RATING	FRESH WATER RATING
TUE 1	3:55 PM	10:59 PM	5:23 AM	10:35 AM	3	8
WED 2	4:55 PM	11:44 PM	5:55 AM	11:21 AM	○ 5	7
THUR 3	5:54 PM		6:24 AM	12:05 PM	7	6
FRI 4	6:52 PM	12:26 AM	6:50 AM	12:46 PM	7	6
SAT 5	7:48 PM	1:07 AM	7:15 AM	1:27 PM	7	6
SUN 6	8:45 PM	1:48 AM	7:39 AM	2:08 PM	5	5
MON 7	9:42 PM	2:29 AM	8:05 AM	2:50 PM	4	4
TUE 8	10:41 PM	3:11 AM	8:33 AM	3:33 PM	3	6
WED 9	11:40 PM	3:55 AM	9:04 AM	4:18 PM	4	4
THUR 10		4:42 AM	9:40 AM	5:07 PM	5	5
FRI 11	12:39 AM	5:32 AM	10:23 AM	5:58 PM	6	6

SEPTEMBER 2020

POPULAR LOCATION ADJUSTMENTS (See full list on page 7)

DAY	MINOR BITE	MAJOR BITE	MINOR BITE	MAJOR BITE	SALT WATER RATING	FRESH WATER RATING
SAT 12	1:37 AM	6:25 AM	11:13 AM	6:52 PM	7	7
SUN 13	2:32 AM	7:20 AM	12:10 PM	7:48 PM	7	8
MON 14	3:22 AM	8:17 AM	1:15 PM	8:45 PM	5	8
TUE 15	4:07 AM	9:13 AM	2:25 PM	9:41 PM	6	7
WED 16	4:48 AM	10:09 AM	3:38 PM	10:36 PM	8	8
THUR 17	5:24 AM	11:03 AM	4:52 PM	11:30 PM	● 8	8
FRI 18	5:57 AM	11:57 AM	6:06 PM		8	6
SAT 19	6:30 AM	12:50 PM	7:20 PM	12:23 AM	7	6
SUN 20	7:03 AM	1:43 PM	8:34 PM	1:16 AM	6	7
MON 21	7:38 AM	2:38 PM	9:47 PM	2:10 AM	5	5
TUE 22	8:17 AM	3:34 PM	10:59 PM	3:06 AM	4	6
WED 23	9:01 AM	4:31 PM		4:02 AM	3	5
THUR 24	9:50 AM	5:28 PM	12:06 AM	4:59 AM	4	6
FRI 25	10:46 AM	6:24 PM	1:08 AM	5:56 AM	5	6
SAT 26	11:45 AM	7:18 PM	2:01 AM	6:50 AM	4	5
SUN 27	12:46 PM	8:09 PM	2:47 AM	7:43 AM	3	5
MON 28	1:48 PM	8:57 PM	3:25 AM	8:33 AM	6	6
TUE 29	2:48 PM	9:42 PM	3:58 AM	9:19 AM	6	6
WED 30	3:47 PM	10:24 PM	4:27 AM	10:03 AM	5	7

Apogee moon phase on Sunday 4th and Saturday 21st
Perigee moon phase on Saturday 17th
● New moon on Saturday 17th
First quarter moon on Friday 23rd
○ Full moon on Friday 2nd
Last quarter moon phase on Saturday 10th

Melbourne, VIC: Rise: 06:30am Set: 07:30pm

Note: Daylight Savings start (clocks turn forward 1 hour) on Sunday, October 4th at 2:00 AM.
Subtract 1 hour to rise/set time for days before October 4th. These sun rise/set times are averages for the month

DAY	MINOR BITE	MAJOR BITE	MINOR BITE	MAJOR BITE	SALT WATER RATING	FRESH WATER RATING
THUR 1	4:45 PM	11:06 PM	4:54 AM	10:45 AM	3	8
FRI 2	5:42 PM	11:46 PM	5:18 AM	11:26 AM	○ 5	7
SAT 3	6:38 PM		5:43 AM	12:06 PM	7	6
SUN 4	7:35 PM	12:27 AM	6:08 AM	12:47 PM	7	6
MON 5	8:33 PM	1:08 AM	6:35 AM	1:30 PM	5	5
TUE 6	9:32 PM	1:52 AM	7:04 AM	2:14 PM	4	4
WED 7	10:31 PM	2:37 AM	7:38 AM	3:01 PM	4	4
THUR 8	11:28 PM	3:26 AM	8:17 AM	3:51 PM	3	6
FRI 9		4:17 AM	9:03 AM	4:43 PM	4	4
SAT 10	12:23 AM	5:10 AM	9:57 AM	5:37 PM	5	5
SUN 11	1:14 AM	6:04 AM	10:57 AM	6:31 PM	6	6

OCTOBER 2020

POPULAR LOCATION ADJUSTMENTS (See full list on page 7)

DAY	MINOR BITE	MAJOR BITE	MINOR BITE	MAJOR BITE	SALT WATER RATING	FRESH WATER RATING
MON 12	2:00 AM	6:59 AM	12:03 PM	7:26 PM	7	7
TUE 13	2:41 AM	7:53 AM	1:13 PM	8:19 PM	7	8
WED 14	3:18 AM	8:47 AM	2:25 PM	9:13 PM	5	8
THUR 15	3:52 AM	9:40 AM	3:38 PM	10:06 PM	6	7
FRI 16	4:24 AM	10:33 AM	4:53 PM	11:00 PM	8	8
SAT 17	4:57 AM	11:27 AM	6:08 PM	11:54 PM	● 8	8
SUN 18	5:32 AM	12:22 PM	7:24 PM		8	6
MON 19	6:09 AM	1:20 PM	8:40 PM	12:51 AM	7	6
TUE 20	6:52 AM	2:19 PM	9:52 PM	1:49 AM	6	7
WED 21	7:41 AM	3:18 PM	10:59 PM	2:48 AM	5	5
THUR 22	8:37 AM	4:17 PM	11:57 PM	3:47 AM	4	6
FRI 23	9:36 AM	5:13 PM		4:45 AM	4	6
SAT 24	10:38 AM	6:06 PM	12:46 AM	5:39 AM	4	6
SUN 25	11:40 AM	6:55 PM	1:27 AM	6:30 AM	5	6
MON 26	12:41 PM	7:41 PM	2:02 AM	7:17 AM	4	5
TUE 27	1:41 PM	8:24 PM	2:32 AM	8:02 AM	3	5
WED 28	2:39 PM	9:05 PM	2:58 AM	8:44 AM	6	6
THUR 29	3:35 PM	9:45 PM	3:23 AM	9:24 AM	5	7
FRI 30	4:32 PM	10:26 PM	3:47 AM	10:05 AM	3	8
SAT 31	5:29 PM	11:07 PM	4:12 AM	10:46 AM	5	7

Apogee moon phase on Friday 27th
Perigee moon phase on Saturday 14th
● New moon on Sunday 15th
First quarter moon on Sunday 22nd
○ Full moon on Sunday 1st and Monday 30th
Last quarter moon phase on Sunday 8th

Melbourne, VIC: Rise: 06:00am Set: 08:10pm

(Note: These sun rise/set times are averages for the month)

DAY	MINOR BITE	MAJOR BITE	MINOR BITE	MAJOR BITE	SALT WATER RATING	FRESH WATER RATING
SUN 1	6:27 PM	11:50 PM	4:38 AM	11:28 AM	○ 5	7
MON 2	7:26 PM		5:07 AM	12:12 PM	7	6
TUE 3	8:25 PM	12:35 AM	5:39 AM	12:58 PM	7	6
WED 4	9:23 PM	1:22 AM	6:16 AM	1:46 PM	5	5
THUR 5	10:19 PM	2:12 AM	7:00 AM	2:37 PM	4	4
FRI 6	11:11 PM	3:04 AM	7:50 AM	3:31 PM	3	6
SAT 7	11:57 PM	3:58 AM	8:47 AM	4:24 PM	4	4
SUN 8		4:51 AM	9:49 AM	5:17 PM	5	5
MON 9	12:38 AM	5:44 AM	10:55 AM	6:10 PM	6	6
TUE 10	1:15 AM	6:36 AM	12:04 PM	7:01 PM	7	7
WED 11	1:49 AM	7:27 AM	1:14 PM	7:52 PM	7	8

POPULAR LOCATION ADJUSTMENTS (See full list on page 7)

DAY	MINOR BITE	MAJOR BITE	MINOR BITE	MAJOR BITE	SALT WATER RATING	FRESH WATER RATING
THUR 12	2:20 AM	8:18 AM	2:26 PM	8:44 PM	5	8
FRI 13	2:52 AM	9:10 AM	3:39 PM	9:37 PM	6	7
SAT 14	3:24 AM	10:04 AM	4:54 PM	10:32 PM	8	8
SUN 15	4:00 AM	11:00 AM	6:11 PM	11:29 PM	● 8	8
MON 16	4:40 AM	11:59 AM	7:27 PM		8	6
TUE 17	5:27 AM	1:00 PM	8:39 PM	12:29 AM	7	6
WED 18	6:21 AM	2:02 PM	9:44 PM	1:30 AM	6	7
THUR 19	7:21 AM	3:02 PM	10:39 PM	2:31 AM	5	5
FRI 20	8:24 AM	3:58 PM	11:25 PM	3:30 AM	4	6
SAT 21	9:29 AM	4:50 PM		4:24 AM	3	5
SUN 22	10:32 AM	5:38 PM	12:03 AM	5:14 AM	4	6
MON 23	11:33 AM	6:22 PM	12:35 AM	6:00 AM	5	6
TUE 24	12:31 PM	7:04 PM	1:03 AM	6:43 AM	4	5
WED 25	1:29 PM	7:45 PM	1:28 AM	7:24 AM	4	5
THUR 26	2:25 PM	8:25 PM	1:52 AM	8:05 AM	3	5
FRI 27	3:22 PM	9:05 PM	2:16 AM	8:45 AM	6	6
SAT 28	4:20 PM	9:48 PM	2:42 AM	9:26 AM	5	7
SUN 29	5:18 PM	10:32 PM	3:09 AM	10:09 AM	3	8
MON 30	6:18 PM	11:19 PM	3:40 AM	10:55 AM	○ 5	7

Apogee moon phase on Friday 25th
Perigee moon phase on Sunday 13th
● **New moon on Tuesday 15th**
First quarter moon on Tuesday 22nd
○ **Full moon on Wednesday 30th**
Last quarter moon phase on Tuesday 8th

Melbourne, VIC: Rise: 05:50am Set: 08:30pm
(Note: These sun rise/set times are averages for the month)

DAY	MINOR BITE	MAJOR BITE	MINOR BITE	MAJOR BITE	SALT WATER RATING	FRESH WATER RATING
TUE 1	7:17 PM		4:16 AM	11:43 AM	7	6
WED 2	8:15 PM	12:09 AM	4:57 AM	12:35 PM	7	6
THUR 3	9:08 PM	1:01 AM	5:46 AM	1:27 PM	7	6
FRI 4	9:56 PM	1:54 AM	6:41 AM	2:20 PM	5	5
SAT 5	10:39 PM	2:47 AM	7:42 AM	3:13 PM	4	4
SUN 6	11:16 PM	3:40 AM	8:46 AM	4:05 PM	3	6
MON 7	11:50 PM	4:31 AM	9:53 AM	4:56 PM	4	4
TUE 8		5:21 AM	11:00 AM	5:45 PM	5	5
WED 9	12:21 AM	6:10 AM	12:09 PM	6:34 PM	6	6
THUR 10	12:51 AM	6:59 AM	1:18 PM	7:24 PM	7	7
FRI 11	1:21 AM	7:50 AM	2:30 PM	8:16 PM	7	8

DECEMBER 2020

POPULAR LOCATION ADJUSTMENTS (See full list on page 7)

DAY	MINOR BITE	MAJOR BITE	MINOR BITE	MAJOR BITE	SALT WATER RATING	FRESH WATER RATING
SAT 12	1:54 AM	8:43 AM	3:44 PM	9:11 PM	5	8
SUN 13	2:30 AM	9:39 AM	4:59 PM	10:08 PM	6	7
MON 14	3:13 AM	10:39 AM	6:13 PM	11:10 PM	8	8
TUE 15	4:03 AM	11:41 AM	7:23 PM		● 8	8
WED 16	5:00 AM	12:43 PM	8:24 PM	12:12 AM	8	6
THUR 17	6:04 AM	1:43 PM	9:16 PM	1:12 AM	7	6
FRI 18	7:10 AM	2:38 PM	9:58 PM	2:10 AM	6	7
SAT 19	8:16 AM	3:30 PM	10:34 PM	3:04 AM	5	5
SUN 20	9:20 AM	4:16 PM	11:04 PM	3:53 AM	4	6
MON 21	10:21 AM	5:00 PM	11:31 PM	4:38 AM	3	5
TUE 22	11:19 AM	5:42 PM	11:55 PM	5:20 AM	4	6
WED 23	12:16 PM	6:22 PM		6:01 AM	5	6
THUR 24	1:13 PM	7:02 PM	12:20 AM	6:42 AM	4	5
FRI 25	2:10 PM	7:44 PM	12:44 AM	7:23 AM	3	5
SAT 26	3:08 PM	8:27 PM	1:11 AM	8:05 AM	6	6
SUN 27	4:08 PM	9:13 PM	1:40 AM	8:50 AM	6	6
MON 28	5:08 PM	10:02 PM	2:14 AM	9:37 AM	5	7
TUE 29	6:06 PM	10:54 PM	2:54 AM	10:28 AM	3	8
WED 30	7:02 PM	11:48 PM	3:40 AM	11:20 AM	○ 5	7
THUR 31	7:53 PM		4:34 AM	12:15 PM	7	6

POPULAR TIDE ADJUSTMENTS

Tamboon Inlet	+ 13mins
Mallacoota Inlet	0
Marlo Bar	+ 25min
Sydenham Inlet (Surf Beach)	+ 15min
Point Hicks	+ 7min
Marlo (Snowy River Entrance)	+ 25min

Eden

(Mallacoota)

Day	Date		Tide 1	
Sun	01		3:26 AM	(0.1) L
Mon	02		4:12 AM	(0.2) L
Tue	03		4:58 AM	(0.3) L
Wed	04		5:46 AM	(0.4) L
Thu	05		12:29 AM	(1.4) **H**
Fri	06		1:34 AM	(1.2) **H**
Sat	07		2:48 AM	(1.1) **H**
Sun	08		4:06 AM	(1.1) **H**
Mon	09		5:13 AM	(1.1) **H**
Tue	10		6:03 AM	(1.1) **H**
Wed	11		12:35 AM	(0.4) L
Thu	12		1:09 AM	(0.3) L
Fri	13		1:40 AM	(0.3) L
Sat	14	○	2:11 AM	(0.3) L
Sun	15		2:42 AM	(0.3) L
Mon	16		3:15 AM	(0.3) L
Tue	17		3:48 AM	(0.4) L
Wed	18		4:22 AM	(0.5) L
Thu	19		4:58 AM	(0.5) L
Fri	20		5:36 AM	(0.6) L
Sat	21		12:39 AM	(1.1) **H**
Sun	22		1:48 AM	(1.1) **H**
Mon	23		3:05 AM	(1.1) **H**
Tue	24		4:16 AM	(1.1) **H**
Wed	25		5:16 AM	(1.2) **H**
Thu	26		6:06 AM	(1.3) **H**
Fri	27		12:43 AM	(0.2) L
Sat	28		1:28 AM	(0.1) L
Sun	29	●	2:12 AM	(0.2) L
Mon	30		2:55 AM	(0.2) L

During Daylight Savings Time add one hour to the times stated below.

SEPTEMBER 2019

Tide 2		Tide 3		Tide 4	
9:34 AM	(1.5) **H**	3:26 PM	(0.3) L	9:45 PM	(1.8) **H**
10:22 AM	(1.5) **H**	4:21 PM	(0.3) L	10:37 PM	(1.7) **H**
11:11 AM	(1.5) **H**	5:20 PM	(0.4) L	11:31 PM	(1.5) **H**
12:02 PM	(1.5) **H**	6:22 PM	(0.4) L		
6:35 AM	(0.5) L	12:57 PM	(1.5) **H**	7:32 PM	(0.5) L
7:28 AM	(0.6) L	1:57 PM	(1.5) **H**	8:47 PM	(0.5) L
8:24 AM	(0.6) L	2:59 PM	(1.4) **H**	10:02 PM	(0.5) L
9:24 AM	(0.7) L	4:01 PM	(1.4) **H**	11:06 PM	(0.5) L
10:22 AM	(0.7) L	4:56 PM	(1.5) **H**	11:56 PM	(0.4) L
11:13 AM	(0.6) L	5:43 PM	(1.5) **H**		
6:41 AM	(1.1) **H**	11:59 AM	(0.6) L	6:24 PM	(1.5) **H**
7:15 AM	(1.2) **H**	12:42 PM	(0.5) L	7:02 PM	(1.5) **H**
7:47 AM	(1.3) **H**	1:23 PM	(0.5) L	7:39 PM	(1.5) **H**
8:20 AM	(1.3) **H**	2:03 PM	(0.5) L	8:16 PM	(1.5) **H**
8:54 AM	(1.4) **H**	2:43 PM	(0.5) L	8:54 PM	(1.5) **H**
9:28 AM	(1.4) **H**	3:24 PM	(0.5) L	9:32 PM	(1.5) **H**
10:04 AM	(1.4) **H**	4:07 PM	(0.5) L	10:12 PM	(1.4) **H**
10:40 AM	(1.4) **H**	4:52 PM	(0.5) L	10:54 PM	(1.3) **H**
11:20 AM	(1.4) **H**	5:43 PM	(0.5) L	11:42 PM	(1.2) **H**
12:04 PM	(1.4) **H**	6:42 PM	(0.6) L		
6:22 AM	(0.6) L	12:55 PM	(1.4) **H**	7:50 PM	(0.5) L
7:20 AM	(0.7) L	1:56 PM	(1.4) **H**	9:01 PM	(0.5) L
8:28 AM	(0.7) L	3:01 PM	(1.5) **H**	10:07 PM	(0.4) L
9:38 AM	(0.6) L	4:07 PM	(1.5) **H**	11:04 PM	(0.3) L
10:44 AM	(0.6) L	5:08 PM	(1.6) **H**	11:55 PM	(0.2) L
11:43 AM	(0.5) L	6:05 PM	(1.7) **H**		
6:53 AM	(1.4) **H**	12:38 PM	(0.4) L	6:58 PM	(1.7) **H**
7:37 AM	(1.5) **H**	1:31 PM	(0.3) L	7:49 PM	(1.8) **H**
8:22 AM	(1.6) **H**	2:24 PM	(0.2) L	8:39 PM	(1.7) **H**
9:06 AM	(1.6) **H**	3:16 PM	(0.2) L	9:30 PM	(1.6) **H**

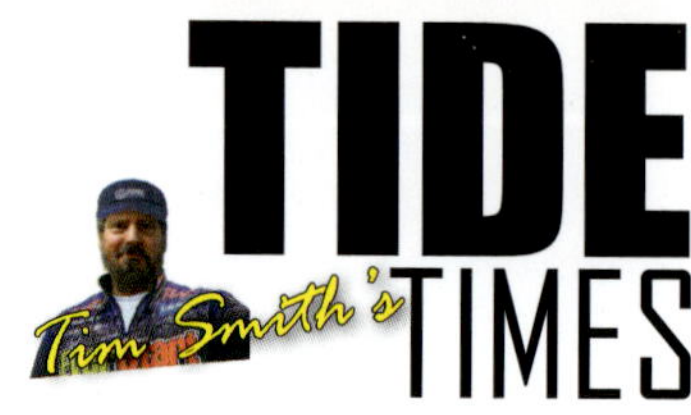

Eden

(Mallacoota)

Day	Date	Tide 1
Tue	01	3:39 AM (0.3) L
Wed	02	4:23 AM (0.4) L
Thu	03	5:08 AM (0.5) L
Fri	04	12:14 AM (1.2) **H**
Sat	05	1:22 AM (1.1) **H**
Sun	06	2:41 AM (1.0) **H**
Mon	07	4:01 AM (1.0) **H**
Tue	08	4:59 AM (1.1) **H**
Wed	09	5:40 AM (1.1) **H**
Thu	10	6:12 AM (1.2) **H**
Fri	11	12:25 AM (0.4) L
Sat	12	12:55 AM (0.4) L
Sun	13	1:26 AM (0.4) L
Mon	14 ○	1:58 AM (0.4) L
Tue	15	2:30 AM (0.4) L
Wed	16	3:04 AM (0.4) L
Thu	17	3:38 AM (0.5) L
Fri	18	4:14 AM (0.6) L
Sat	19	4:55 AM (0.6) L
Sun	20	12:29 AM (1.1) **H**
Mon	21	1:41 AM (1.1) **H**
Tue	22	2:55 AM (1.1) **H**
Wed	23	4:01 AM (1.2) **H**
Thu	24	4:56 AM (1.3) **H**
Fri	25	5:45 AM (1.4) **H**
Sat	26	12:14 AM (0.2) L
Sun	27	12:58 AM (0.2) L
Mon	28 ●	1:42 AM (0.3) L
Tue	29	2:24 AM (0.3) L
Wed	30	3:06 AM (0.4) L
Thu	31	3:47 AM (0.5) L

POPULAR TIDE ADJUSTMENTS

Location	Adjustment
Tamboon Inlet	+ 13mins
Mallacoota Inlet	0
Marlo Bar	+ 25min
Sydenham Inlet (Surf Beach)	+ 15min
Point Hicks	+ 7min
Marlo (Snowy River Entrance)	+ 25min

During Daylight Savings Time add one hour to the times stated below.

OCTOBER 2019

Tide 2		Tide 3		Tide 4	
9:52 AM	(1.6) **H**	4:10 PM	(0.2) L	10:21 PM	(1.5) **H**
10:38 AM	(1.6) **H**	5:07 PM	(0.3) L	11:15 PM	(1.4) **H**
11:27 AM	(1.6) **H**	6:08 PM	(0.4) L		
5:55 AM	(0.6) L	12:20 PM	(1.5) **H**	7:15 PM	(0.4) L
6:48 AM	(0.7) L	1:17 PM	(1.4) **H**	8:28 PM	(0.5) L
7:49 AM	(0.7) L	2:20 PM	(1.4) **H**	9:38 PM	(0.5) L
8:57 AM	(0.8) L	3:24 PM	(1.4) **H**	10:35 PM	(0.5) L
10:02 AM	(0.7) L	4:21 PM	(1.4) **H**	11:19 PM	(0.4) L
10:56 AM	(0.7) L	5:09 PM	(1.4) **H**	11:54 PM	(0.4) L
11:42 AM	(0.6) L	5:51 PM	(1.4) **H**		
6:42 AM	(1.3) **H**	12:24 PM	(0.6) L	6:31 PM	(1.5) **H**
7:12 AM	(1.4) **H**	1:04 PM	(0.5) L	7:09 PM	(1.5) **H**
7:43 AM	(1.5) **H**	1:43 PM	(0.5) L	7:47 PM	(1.5) **H**
8:16 AM	(1.5) **H**	2:23 PM	(0.4) L	8:26 PM	(1.5) **H**
8:49 AM	(1.6) **H**	3:04 PM	(0.4) L	9:06 PM	(1.4) **H**
9:24 AM	(1.6) **H**	3:47 PM	(0.4) L	9:48 PM	(1.3) **H**
10:00 AM	(1.6) **H**	4:33 PM	(0.4) L	10:35 PM	(1.3) **H**
10:40 AM	(1.5) **H**	5:25 PM	(0.4) L	11:27 PM	(1.2) **H**
11:26 AM	(1.5) **H**	6:24 PM	(0.4) L		
5:47 AM	(0.7) L	12:21 PM	(1.5) **H**	7:29 PM	(0.4) L
6:54 AM	(0.7) L	1:25 PM	(1.5) **H**	8:37 PM	(0.4) L
8:11 AM	(0.7) L	2:35 PM	(1.5) **H**	9:40 PM	(0.3) L
9:27 AM	(0.7) L	3:44 PM	(1.6) **H**	10:36 PM	(0.3) L
10:34 AM	(0.6) L	4:49 PM	(1.6) **H**	11:27 PM	(0.3) L
11:35 AM	(0.5) L	5:47 PM	(1.7) **H**		
6:30 AM	(1.6) **H**	12:30 PM	(0.3) L	6:42 PM	(1.7) **H**
7:14 AM	(1.7) **H**	1:23 PM	(0.3) L	7:34 PM	(1.7) **H**
7:57 AM	(1.7) **H**	2:15 PM	(0.2) L	8:25 PM	(1.6) **H**
8:41 AM	(1.8) **H**	3:07 PM	(0.2) L	9:15 PM	(1.5) **H**
9:25 AM	(1.7) **H**	4:00 PM	(0.2) L	10:07 PM	(1.4) **H**
10:09 AM	(1.7) **H**	4:55 PM	(0.3) L	11:01 PM	(1.2) **H**

POPULAR TIDE ADJUSTMENTS

Tamboon Inlet	+ 13mins
Mallacoota Inlet	0
Marlo Bar	+ 25min
Sydenham Inlet (Surf Beach)	+ 15min
Point Hicks	+ 7min
Marlo (Snowy River Entrance)	+ 25min

Eden

(Mallacoota)

Day	Date		Tide 1
Fri	01		4:30 AM (0.6) L
Sat	02		5:15 AM (0.7) L
Sun	03		1:06 AM (1.0) **H**
Mon	04		2:21 AM (1.0) **H**
Tue	05		3:33 AM (1.1) **H**
Wed	06		4:26 AM (1.1) **H**
Thu	07		5:03 AM (1.2) **H**
Fri	08		5:35 AM (1.3) **H**
Sat	09		6:05 AM (1.4) **H**
Sun	10		12:09 AM (0.4) L
Mon	11		12:42 AM (0.4) L
Tue	12	○	1:16 AM (0.4) L
Wed	13		1:50 AM (0.5) L
Thu	14		2:25 AM (0.5) L
Fri	15		3:02 AM (0.5) L
Sat	16		3:43 AM (0.6) L
Sun	17		4:30 AM (0.6) L
Mon	18		12:19 AM (1.1) **H**
Tue	19		1:26 AM (1.1) **H**
Wed	20		2:33 AM (1.2) **H**
Thu	21		3:35 AM (1.3) **H**
Fri	22		4:30 AM (1.4) **H**
Sat	23		5:20 AM (1.6) **H**
Sun	24		6:07 AM (1.7) **H**
Mon	25		12:29 AM (0.3) L
Tue	26		1:13 AM (0.4) L
Wed	27	●	1:55 AM (0.4) L
Thu	28		2:36 AM (0.5) L
Fri	29		3:16 AM (0.5) L
Sat	30		3:58 AM (0.6) L

NOVEMBER 2019

During Daylight Savings Time add one hour to the times stated below.

Tide 2		Tide 3		Tide 4	
10:55 AM	(1.6) **H**	5:52 PM	(0.3) L	11:59 PM	(1.1) **H**
11:44 AM	(1.5) **H**	6:53 PM	(0.4) L		
6:07 AM	(0.7) L	12:36 PM	(1.4) **H**	7:56 PM	(0.4) L
7:10 AM	(0.8) L	1:34 PM	(1.4) **H**	8:56 PM	(0.5) L
8:22 AM	(0.8) L	2:34 PM	(1.3) **H**	9:47 PM	(0.5) L
9:32 AM	(0.8) L	3:32 PM	(1.3) **H**	10:28 PM	(0.5) L
10:31 AM	(0.8) L	4:25 PM	(1.3) **H**	11:03 PM	(0.5) L
11:19 AM	(0.7) L	5:12 PM	(1.4) **H**	11:36 PM	(0.5) L
12:03 PM	(0.6) L	5:55 PM	(1.4) **H**		
6:36 AM	(1.5) **H**	12:44 PM	(0.6) L	6:37 PM	(1.4) **H**
7:08 AM	(1.6) **H**	1:24 PM	(0.5) L	7:19 PM	(1.4) **H**
7:41 AM	(1.6) **H**	2:05 PM	(0.4) L	8:02 PM	(1.4) **H**
8:16 AM	(1.7) **H**	2:47 PM	(0.4) L	8:45 PM	(1.3) **H**
8:52 AM	(1.7) **H**	3:32 PM	(0.3) L	9:32 PM	(1.3) **H**
9:31 AM	(1.7) **H**	4:19 PM	(0.3) L	10:22 PM	(1.2) **H**
10:13 AM	(1.7) **H**	5:11 PM	(0.3) L	11:17 PM	(1.1) **H**
11:02 AM	(1.6) **H**	6:07 PM	(0.3) L		
5:27 AM	(0.7) L	11:58 AM	(1.6) **H**	7:08 PM	(0.3) L
6:37 AM	(0.7) L	1:02 PM	(1.6) **H**	8:09 PM	(0.3) L
7:55 AM	(0.7) L	2:11 PM	(1.6) **H**	9:09 PM	(0.3) L
9:12 AM	(0.7) L	3:21 PM	(1.6) **H**	10:05 PM	(0.3) L
10:22 AM	(0.6) L	4:28 PM	(1.6) **H**	10:56 PM	(0.3) L
11:25 AM	(0.5) L	5:30 PM	(1.6) **H**	11:44 PM	(0.3) L
12:22 PM	(0.4) L	6:27 PM	(1.5) **H**		
6:52 AM	(1.8) **H**	1:17 PM	(0.3) L	7:21 PM	(1.5) **H**
7:36 AM	(1.8) **H**	2:09 PM	(0.2) L	8:12 PM	(1.4) **H**
8:19 AM	(1.8) **H**	3:00 PM	(0.2) L	9:03 PM	(1.3) **H**
9:02 AM	(1.8) **H**	3:51 PM	(0.2) L	9:54 PM	(1.2) **H**
9:45 AM	(1.7) **H**	4:41 PM	(0.2) L	10:45 PM	(1.1) **H**
10:28 AM	(1.6) **H**	5:32 PM	(0.3) L	11:39 PM	(1.1) **H**

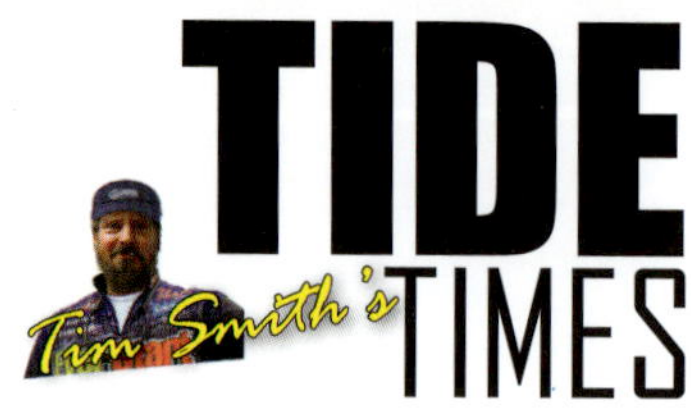

POPULAR TIDE ADJUSTMENTS

Tamboon Inlet	+ 13mins
Mallacoota Inlet	0
Marlo Bar	+ 25min
Sydenham Inlet (Surf Beach)	+ 15min
Point Hicks	+ 7min
Marlo (Snowy River Entrance)	+ 25min

Eden
(Mallacoota)

Day	Date		Tide 1
Sun	01		4:41 AM (0.7) L
Mon	02		12:37 AM (1.1) **H**
Tue	03		1:38 AM (1.1) **H**
Wed	04		2:38 AM (1.1) **H**
Thu	05		3:30 AM (1.2) **H**
Fri	06		4:13 AM (1.3) **H**
Sat	07		4:51 AM (1.4) **H**
Sun	08		5:26 AM (1.5) **H**
Mon	09		6:00 AM (1.6) **H**
Tue	10		12:00 AM (0.5) L
Wed	11		12:38 AM (0.5) L
Thu	12	○	1:16 AM (0.5) L
Fri	13		1:56 AM (0.5) L
Sat	14		2:39 AM (0.5) L
Sun	15		3:25 AM (0.5) L
Mon	16		4:17 AM (0.6) L
Tue	17		12:00 AM (1.2) **H**
Wed	18		1:00 AM (1.2) **H**
Thu	19		2:02 AM (1.3) **H**
Fri	20		3:02 AM (1.4) **H**
Sat	21		4:00 AM (1.5) **H**
Sun	22		4:54 AM (1.6) **H**
Mon	23		5:45 AM (1.7) **H**
Tue	24		12:02 AM (0.4) L
Wed	25		12:47 AM (0.5) L
Thu	26	●	1:30 AM (0.5) L
Fri	27		2:11 AM (0.5) L
Sat	28		2:52 AM (0.5) L
Sun	29		3:34 AM (0.6) L
Mon	30		4:16 AM (0.6) L
Tue	31		5:03 AM (0.7) L

During Daylight Savings Time add one hour to the times stated below.

DECEMBER 2019

Tide 2		Tide 3		Tide 4	
11:12 AM	(1.5) **H**	6:22 PM	(0.4) L		
5:31 AM	(0.7) L	11:57 AM	(1.5) **H**	7:12 PM	(0.4) L
6:29 AM	(0.8) L	12:46 PM	(1.4) **H**	8:01 PM	(0.5) L
7:38 AM	(0.9) L	1:39 PM	(1.3) **H**	8:46 PM	(0.5) L
8:48 AM	(0.9) L	2:35 PM	(1.3) **H**	9:28 PM	(0.5) L
9:53 AM	(0.8) L	3:32 PM	(1.3) **H**	10:08 PM	(0.5) L
10:49 AM	(0.8) L	4:27 PM	(1.3) **H**	10:46 PM	(0.5) L
11:38 AM	(0.7) L	5:18 PM	(1.3) **H**	11:23 PM	(0.5) L
12:23 PM	(0.6) L	6:08 PM	(1.3) **H**		
6:35 AM	(1.6) **H**	1:06 PM	(0.5) L	6:55 PM	(1.3) **H**
7:11 AM	(1.7) **H**	1:49 PM	(0.4) L	7:43 PM	(1.3) **H**
7:48 AM	(1.7) **H**	2:33 PM	(0.3) L	8:30 PM	(1.2) **H**
8:28 AM	(1.8) **H**	3:19 PM	(0.2) L	9:19 PM	(1.2) **H**
9:11 AM	(1.8) **H**	4:06 PM	(0.2) L	10:10 PM	(1.2) **H**
9:57 AM	(1.8) **H**	4:56 PM	(0.2) L	11:03 PM	(1.2) **H**
10:47 AM	(1.7) **H**	5:48 PM	(0.2) L		
5:17 AM	(0.6) L	11:43 AM	(1.7) **H**	6:43 PM	(0.2) L
6:24 AM	(0.6) L	12:43 PM	(1.6) **H**	7:39 PM	(0.3) L
7:38 AM	(0.7) L	1:49 PM	(1.6) **H**	8:36 PM	(0.3) L
8:54 AM	(0.6) L	2:58 PM	(1.5) **H**	9:31 PM	(0.4) L
10:07 AM	(0.6) L	4:07 PM	(1.5) **H**	10:24 PM	(0.4) L
11:15 AM	(0.5) L	5:13 PM	(1.4) **H**	11:14 PM	(0.4) L
12:16 PM	(0.4) L	6:14 PM	(1.4) **H**		
6:32 AM	(1.8) **H**	1:12 PM	(0.3) L	7:11 PM	(1.3) **H**
7:17 AM	(1.8) **H**	2:03 PM	(0.2) L	8:02 PM	(1.3) **H**
8:01 AM	(1.8) **H**	2:52 PM	(0.2) L	8:51 PM	(1.2) **H**
8:43 AM	(1.8) **H**	3:37 PM	(0.2) L	9:38 PM	(1.2) **H**
9:24 AM	(1.7) **H**	4:21 PM	(0.2) L	10:24 PM	(1.1) **H**
10:04 AM	(1.6) **H**	5:03 PM	(0.3) L	11:09 PM	(1.1) **H**
10:43 AM	(1.6) **H**	5:43 PM	(0.3) L	11:55 PM	(1.1) **H**
11:23 AM	(1.5) **H**	6:23 PM	(0.4) L		

POPULAR TIDE ADJUSTMENTS

Tamboon Inlet	+ 13mins
Mallacoota Inlet	0
Marlo Bar	+ 25min
Sydenham Inlet (Surf Beach)	+ 15min
Point Hicks	+ 7min
Marlo (Snowy River Entrance)	+ 25min

Eden

(Mallacoota)

Day	Date		Tide 1
Wed	1		12:47 AM (1.1) **H**
Thu	2		1:36 AM (1.2) **H**
Fri	3		2:25 AM (1.3) **H**
Sat	4		3:13 AM (1.3) **H**
Sun	5		3:58 AM (1.4) **H**
Mon	6		4:41 AM (1.5) **H**
Tue	7		5:22 AM (1.5) **H**
Wed	8		6:03 AM (1.6) **H**
Thu	9		12:06 AM (0.5) L
Fri	10		12:51 AM (0.5) L
Sat	11	○	1:37 AM (0.5) L
Sun	12		2:25 AM (0.5) L
Mon	13		3:15 AM (0.5) L
Tue	14		4:09 AM (0.5) L
Wed	15		5:07 AM (0.5) L
Thu	16		12:29 AM (1.4) **H**
Fri	17		1:26 AM (1.4) **H**
Sat	18		2:26 AM (1.5) **H**
Sun	19		3:26 AM (1.5) **H**
Mon	20		4:26 AM (1.6) **H**
Tue	21		5:22 AM (1.7) **H**
Wed	22		6:13 AM (1.7) **H**
Thu	23		12:24 AM (0.5) L
Fri	24		1:09 AM (0.5) L
Sat	25	●	1:52 AM (0.5) L
Sun	26		2:33 AM (0.5) L
Mon	27		3:14 AM (0.5) L
Tue	28		3:56 AM (0.6) L
Wed	29		4:39 AM (0.6) L
Thu	30		5:25 AM (0.7) L
Fri	31		12:35 AM (1.3) **H**

During Daylight Savings Time add one hour to the times stated below.

JANUARY 2020

Tide 2		Tide 3		Tide 4	
5:54 AM	(0.8) L	12:06 PM	(1.4) **H**	7:06 PM	(0.5) L
6:54 AM	(0.8) L	12:51 PM	(1.4) **H**	7:46 PM	(0.5) L
8:00 AM	(0.9) L	1:42 PM	(1.3) **H**	8:28 PM	(0.6) L
9:08 AM	(0.8) L	2:39 PM	(1.2) **H**	9:10 PM	(0.6) L
10:13 AM	(0.8) L	3:41 PM	(1.2) **H**	9:54 PM	(0.6) L
11:11 AM	(0.7) L	4:44 PM	(1.2) **H**	10:37 PM	(0.6) L
12:03 PM	(0.6) L	5:43 PM	(1.2) **H**	11:21 PM	(0.6) L
12:50 PM	(0.5) L	6:38 PM	(1.2) **H**		
6:44 AM	(1.7) **H**	1:36 PM	(0.3) L	7:30 PM	(1.2) **H**
7:27 AM	(1.7) **H**	2:20 PM	(0.2) L	8:19 PM	(1.2) **H**
8:11 AM	(1.8) **H**	3:05 PM	(0.2) L	9:07 PM	(1.2) **H**
8:57 AM	(1.8) **H**	3:51 PM	(0.1) L	9:55 PM	(1.2) **H**
9:45 AM	(1.8) **H**	4:37 PM	(0.1) L	10:45 PM	(1.3) **H**
10:35 AM	(1.8) **H**	5:25 PM	(0.2) L	11:36 PM	(1.3) **H**
11:28 AM	(1.7) **H**	6:15 PM	(0.2) L		
6:10 AM	(0.6) L	12:26 PM	(1.6) **H**	7:07 PM	(0.3) L
7:20 AM	(0.6) L	1:28 PM	(1.5) **H**	8:00 PM	(0.4) L
8:35 AM	(0.6) L	2:36 PM	(1.4) **H**	8:55 PM	(0.5) L
9:53 AM	(0.6) L	3:49 PM	(1.3) **H**	9:50 PM	(0.5) L
11:06 AM	(0.5) L	5:02 PM	(1.2) **H**	10:45 PM	(0.5) L
12:11 PM	(0.4) L	6:08 PM	(1.2) **H**	11:36 PM	(0.5) L
1:07 PM	(0.3) L	7:05 PM	(1.2) **H**		
7:00 AM	(1.7) **H**	1:56 PM	(0.3) L	7:55 PM	(1.1) **H**
7:44 AM	(1.7) **H**	2:39 PM	(0.2) L	8:38 PM	(1.1) **H**
8:24 AM	(1.7) **H**	3:18 PM	(0.2) L	9:19 PM	(1.1) **H**
9:03 AM	(1.7) **H**	3:54 PM	(0.2) L	9:57 PM	(1.2) **H**
9:40 AM	(1.6) **H**	4:29 PM	(0.3) L	10:35 PM	(1.2) **H**
10:16 AM	(1.6) **H**	5:02 PM	(0.3) L	11:13 PM	(1.2) **H**
10:53 AM	(1.5) **H**	5:36 PM	(0.4) L	11:53 PM	(1.3) **H**
11:31 AM	(1.4) **H**	6:11 PM	(0.5) L		
6:16 AM	(0.8) L	12:12 PM	(1.4) **H**	6:48 PM	(0.5) L

POPULAR TIDE ADJUSTMENTS

Location	Adjustment
Tamboon Inlet	+ 13mins
Mallacoota Inlet	0
Marlo Bar	+ 25min
Sydenham Inlet (Surf Beach)	+ 15min
Point Hicks	+ 7min
Marlo (Snowy River Entrance)	+ 25min

Eden

(Mallacoota)

Day	Date		Tide 1
Sat	1		1:19 AM (1.3) **H**
Sun	2		2:07 AM (1.3) **H**
Mon	3		2:58 AM (1.4) **H**
Tue	4		3:50 AM (1.4) **H**
Wed	5		4:42 AM (1.5) **H**
Thu	6		5:32 AM (1.6) **H**
Fri	7		6:21 AM (1.7) **H**
Sat	8		12:35 AM (0.5) L
Sun	9	○	1:26 AM (0.4) L
Mon	10		2:17 AM (0.4) L
Tue	11		3:08 AM (0.4) L
Wed	12		4:02 AM (0.4) L
Thu	13		4:57 AM (0.4) L
Fri	14		5:58 AM (0.5) L
Sat	15		12:50 AM (1.5) **H**
Sun	16		1:49 AM (1.5) **H**
Mon	17		2:53 AM (1.5) **H**
Tue	18		3:58 AM (1.5) **H**
Wed	19		5:00 AM (1.6) **H**
Thu	20		5:55 AM (1.6) **H**
Fri	21		12:09 AM (0.6) L
Sat	22		12:55 AM (0.6) L
Sun	23		1:37 AM (0.5) L
Mon	24	●	2:17 AM (0.5) L
Tue	25		2:57 AM (0.5) L
Wed	26		3:36 AM (0.5) L
Thu	27		4:17 AM (0.6) L
Fri	28		5:00 AM (0.6) L
Sat	29		5:47 AM (0.7) L

During Daylight Savings Time add one hour to the times stated below.

FEBRUARY 2020

Tide 2		Tide 3		Tide 4	
7:14 AM	(0.8) L	12:59 PM	(1.3) **H**	7:28 PM	(0.6) L
8:21 AM	(0.8) L	1:55 PM	(1.2) **H**	8:12 PM	(0.6) L
9:33 AM	(0.7) L	3:03 PM	(1.1) **H**	9:02 PM	(0.7) L
10:41 AM	(0.7) L	4:17 PM	(1.1) **H**	9:55 PM	(0.6) L
11:40 AM	(0.5) L	5:27 PM	(1.1) **H**	10:50 PM	(0.6) L
12:31 PM	(0.4) L	6:25 PM	(1.1) **H**	11:43 PM	(0.6) L
1:17 PM	(0.3) L	7:16 PM	(1.2) **H**		
7:09 AM	(1.7) **H**	2:01 PM	(0.2) L	8:03 PM	(1.2) **H**
7:57 AM	(1.8) **H**	2:44 PM	(0.1) L	8:48 PM	(1.3) **H**
8:44 AM	(1.9) **H**	3:28 PM	(0.1) L	9:33 PM	(1.4) **H**
9:33 AM	(1.8) **H**	4:12 PM	(0.1) L	10:19 PM	(1.4) **H**
10:23 AM	(1.8) **H**	4:57 PM	(0.2) L	11:06 PM	(1.5) **H**
11:15 AM	(1.7) **H**	5:44 PM	(0.3) L	11:57 PM	(1.5) **H**
12:10 PM	(1.6) **H**	6:32 PM	(0.4) L		
7:04 AM	(0.5) L	1:10 PM	(1.4) **H**	7:24 PM	(0.5) L
8:19 AM	(0.5) L	2:19 PM	(1.3) **H**	8:20 PM	(0.6) L
9:40 AM	(0.5) L	3:38 PM	(1.2) **H**	9:19 PM	(0.6) L
10:58 AM	(0.5) L	4:58 PM	(1.1) **H**	10:20 PM	(0.6) L
12:02 PM	(0.4) L	6:05 PM	(1.1) **H**	11:18 PM	(0.6) L
12:54 PM	(0.4) L	6:57 PM	(1.1) **H**		
6:42 AM	(1.6) **H**	1:36 PM	(0.3) L	7:39 PM	(1.1) **H**
7:24 AM	(1.6) **H**	2:12 PM	(0.3) L	8:15 PM	(1.2) **H**
8:02 AM	(1.6) **H**	2:45 PM	(0.3) L	8:48 PM	(1.2) **H**
8:38 AM	(1.6) **H**	3:16 PM	(0.3) L	9:21 PM	(1.3) **H**
9:14 AM	(1.6) **H**	3:46 PM	(0.3) L	9:55 PM	(1.3) **H**
9:49 AM	(1.6) **H**	4:17 PM	(0.4) L	10:29 PM	(1.4) **H**
10:25 AM	(1.5) **H**	4:49 PM	(0.4) L	11:05 PM	(1.4) **H**
11:03 AM	(1.4) **H**	5:22 PM	(0.5) L	11:43 PM	(1.4) **H**
11:43 AM	(1.3) **H**	5:57 PM	(0.6) L		

POPULAR TIDE ADJUSTMENTS

Tamboon Inlet	+ 13mins
Mallacoota Inlet	0
Marlo Bar	+ 25min
Sydenham Inlet (Surf Beach)	+ 15min
Point Hicks	+ 7min
Marlo (Snowy River Entrance)	+ 25min

Eden

(Mallacoota)

Day	Date		Tide 1		
Sun	1		12:23 AM	(1.4)	**H**
Mon	2		1:09 AM	(1.4)	**H**
Tue	3		2:01 AM	(1.4)	**H**
Wed	4		3:01 AM	(1.4)	**H**
Thu	5		4:04 AM	(1.5)	**H**
Fri	6		5:04 AM	(1.6)	**H**
Sat	7		5:59 AM	(1.7)	**H**
Sun	8		12:25 AM	(0.5)	L
Mon	9		1:17 AM	(0.4)	L
Tue	10	○	2:09 AM	(0.3)	L
Wed	11		3:01 AM	(0.3)	L
Thu	12		3:53 AM	(0.3)	L
Fri	13		4:48 AM	(0.3)	L
Sat	14		5:47 AM	(0.4)	L
Sun	15		12:18 AM	(1.6)	**H**
Mon	16		1:15 AM	(1.6)	**H**
Tue	17		2:19 AM	(1.5)	**H**
Wed	18		3:28 AM	(1.5)	**H**
Thu	19		4:34 AM	(1.5)	**H**
Fri	20		5:29 AM	(1.5)	**H**
Sat	21		6:16 AM	(1.5)	**H**
Sun	22		12:38 AM	(0.6)	L
Mon	23		1:19 AM	(0.6)	L
Tue	24	●	1:58 AM	(0.5)	L
Wed	25		2:37 AM	(0.5)	L
Thu	26		3:17 AM	(0.5)	L
Fri	27		3:57 AM	(0.5)	L
Sat	28		4:40 AM	(0.5)	L
Sun	29		5:26 AM	(0.6)	L
Mon	30		6:19 AM	(0.6)	L
Tue	31		12:24 AM	(1.5)	**H**

During Daylight Savings Time add one hour to the times stated below.

MARCH 2020

Tide 2		Tide 3		Tide 4	
6:41 AM	(0.7) L	12:30 PM	(1.2) **H**	6:35 PM	(0.6) L
7:45 AM	(0.7) L	1:28 PM	(1.1) **H**	7:20 PM	(0.7) L
8:57 AM	(0.7) L	2:41 PM	(1.1) **H**	8:17 PM	(0.7) L
10:09 AM	(0.6) L	4:03 PM	(1.1) **H**	9:22 PM	(0.7) L
11:11 AM	(0.5) L	5:13 PM	(1.1) **H**	10:28 PM	(0.7) L
12:04 PM	(0.4) L	6:09 PM	(1.2) **H**	11:29 PM	(0.6) L
12:50 PM	(0.3) L	6:56 PM	(1.3) **H**		
6:51 AM	(1.8) **H**	1:34 PM	(0.2) L	7:40 PM	(1.4) **H**
7:41 AM	(1.8) **H**	2:17 PM	(0.2) L	8:23 PM	(1.5) **H**
8:31 AM	(1.8) **H**	3:00 PM	(0.2) L	9:07 PM	(1.6) **H**
9:20 AM	(1.8) **H**	3:43 PM	(0.2) L	9:51 PM	(1.6) **H**
10:10 AM	(1.7) **H**	4:27 PM	(0.3) L	10:37 PM	(1.6) **H**
11:02 AM	(1.6) **H**	5:12 PM	(0.4) L	11:26 PM	(1.6) **H**
11:57 AM	(1.5) **H**	5:59 PM	(0.5) L		
6:53 AM	(0.4) L	12:59 PM	(1.3) **H**	6:49 PM	(0.6) L
8:07 AM	(0.5) L	2:11 PM	(1.2) **H**	7:47 PM	(0.7) L
9:26 AM	(0.5) L	3:36 PM	(1.1) **H**	8:52 PM	(0.7) L
10:41 AM	(0.5) L	4:56 PM	(1.1) **H**	10:00 PM	(0.7) L
11:40 AM	(0.4) L	5:55 PM	(1.1) **H**	11:02 PM	(0.7) L
12:25 PM	(0.4) L	6:37 PM	(1.2) **H**	11:54 PM	(0.7) L
1:01 PM	(0.4) L	7:11 PM	(1.2) **H**		
6:56 AM	(1.6) **H**	1:32 PM	(0.4) L	7:41 PM	(1.3) **H**
7:34 AM	(1.6) **H**	2:01 PM	(0.4) L	8:11 PM	(1.4) **H**
8:10 AM	(1.6) **H**	2:31 PM	(0.4) L	8:43 PM	(1.5) **H**
8:46 AM	(1.6) **H**	3:01 PM	(0.4) L	9:15 PM	(1.5) **H**
9:22 AM	(1.5) **H**	3:32 PM	(0.5) L	9:48 PM	(1.5) **H**
10:00 AM	(1.5) **H**	4:04 PM	(0.5) L	10:23 PM	(1.5) **H**
10:40 AM	(1.4) **H**	4:37 PM	(0.6) L	10:59 PM	(1.5) **H**
11:25 AM	(1.3) **H**	5:11 PM	(0.6) L	11:38 PM	(1.5) **H**
12:16 PM	(1.2) **H**	5:51 PM	(0.7) L		
7:21 AM	(0.6) L	1:19 PM	(1.1) **H**	6:40 PM	(0.8) L

Eden

(Mallacoota)

Day	Date	Tide 1
Wed	1	1:18 AM (1.5) **H**
Thu	2	2:22 AM (1.5) **H**
Fri	3	3:31 AM (1.5) **H**
Sat	4	4:36 AM (1.6) **H**
Sun	5	5:36 AM (1.7) **H**
Mon	6	12:13 AM (0.5) L
Tue	7	1:07 AM (0.4) L
Wed	8 ○	2:00 AM (0.3) L
Thu	9	2:52 AM (0.3) L
Fri	10	3:46 AM (0.3) L
Sat	11	4:41 AM (0.3) L
Sun	12	5:40 AM (0.3) L
Mon	13	6:44 AM (0.4) L
Tue	14	12:45 AM (1.6) **H**
Wed	15	1:46 AM (1.5) **H**
Thu	16	2:52 AM (1.5) **H**
Fri	17	3:56 AM (1.4) **H**
Sat	18	4:51 AM (1.4) **H**
Sun	19	5:38 AM (1.5) **H**
Mon	20	12:17 AM (0.7) L
Tue	21	12:57 AM (0.6) L
Wed	22	1:37 AM (0.6) L
Thu	23 ●	2:17 AM (0.5) L
Fri	24	2:57 AM (0.5) L
Sat	25	3:39 AM (0.5) L
Sun	26	4:24 AM (0.5) L
Mon	27	5:12 AM (0.5) L
Tue	28	6:05 AM (0.5) L
Wed	29	7:03 AM (0.5) L
Thu	30	12:50 AM (1.6) **H**

POPULAR TIDE ADJUSTMENTS

Location	Adjustment
Tamboon Inlet	+ 13mins
Mallacoota Inlet	0
Marlo Bar	+ 25min
Sydenham Inlet (Surf Beach)	+ 15min
Point Hicks	+ 7min
Marlo (Snowy River Entrance)	+ 25min

During Daylight Savings Time add one hour to the times stated below.

APRIL 2020

Tide 2		Tide 3		Tide 4	
8:29 AM	(0.6) L	2:34 PM	(1.1) **H**	7:45 PM	(0.8) L
9:37 AM	(0.5) L	3:50 PM	(1.1) **H**	9:00 PM	(0.8) L
10:37 AM	(0.4) L	4:53 PM	(1.2) **H**	10:12 PM	(0.7) L
11:30 AM	(0.4) L	5:44 PM	(1.3) **H**	11:16 PM	(0.6) L
12:17 PM	(0.3) L	6:30 PM	(1.4) **H**		
6:32 AM	(1.7) **H**	1:02 PM	(0.3) L	7:13 PM	(1.6) **H**
7:24 AM	(1.8) **H**	1:46 PM	(0.3) L	7:56 PM	(1.7) **H**
8:15 AM	(1.8) **H**	2:29 PM	(0.3) L	8:40 PM	(1.7) **H**
9:06 AM	(1.7) **H**	3:12 PM	(0.3) L	9:25 PM	(1.8) **H**
9:58 AM	(1.6) **H**	3:56 PM	(0.4) L	10:11 PM	(1.8) **H**
10:51 AM	(1.5) **H**	4:40 PM	(0.5) L	10:59 PM	(1.7) **H**
11:49 AM	(1.3) **H**	5:27 PM	(0.6) L	11:50 PM	(1.7) **H**
12:53 PM	(1.2) **H**	6:18 PM	(0.7) L		
7:53 AM	(0.4) L	2:08 PM	(1.1) **H**	7:17 PM	(0.8) L
9:04 AM	(0.5) L	3:30 PM	(1.1) **H**	8:26 PM	(0.8) L
10:09 AM	(0.5) L	4:39 PM	(1.1) **H**	9:38 PM	(0.8) L
10:59 AM	(0.5) L	5:27 PM	(1.2) **H**	10:41 PM	(0.8) L
11:39 AM	(0.5) L	6:02 PM	(1.3) **H**	11:32 PM	(0.8) L
12:12 PM	(0.5) L	6:32 PM	(1.4) **H**		
6:20 AM	(1.5) **H**	12:42 PM	(0.5) L	7:02 PM	(1.5) **H**
6:59 AM	(1.5) **H**	1:12 PM	(0.5) L	7:32 PM	(1.6) **H**
7:38 AM	(1.5) **H**	1:43 PM	(0.5) L	8:04 PM	(1.6) **H**
8:17 AM	(1.5) **H**	2:15 PM	(0.5) L	8:37 PM	(1.7) **H**
8:57 AM	(1.4) **H**	2:48 PM	(0.5) L	9:11 PM	(1.7) **H**
9:39 AM	(1.4) **H**	3:22 PM	(0.6) L	9:46 PM	(1.7) **H**
10:24 AM	(1.3) **H**	3:57 PM	(0.6) L	10:24 PM	(1.6) **H**
11:14 AM	(1.2) **H**	4:35 PM	(0.7) L	11:05 PM	(1.6) **H**
12:10 PM	(1.2) **H**	5:20 PM	(0.8) L	11:53 PM	(1.6) **H**
1:14 PM	(1.1) **H**	6:17 PM	(0.8) L		
8:04 AM	(0.5) L	2:23 PM	(1.2) **H**	7:29 PM	(0.8) L

POPULAR TIDE ADJUSTMENTS

Tamboon Inlet	+ 13mins
Mallacoota Inlet	0
Marlo Bar	+ 25min
Sydenham Inlet (Surf Beach)	+ 15min
Point Hicks	+ 7min
Marlo (Snowy River Entrance)	+ 25min

Eden

(Mallacoota)

Day	Date	Tide 1
Fri	1	1:54 AM (1.6) **H**
Sat	2	3:03 AM (1.6) **H**
Sun	3	4:10 AM (1.6) **H**
Mon	4	5:12 AM (1.7) **H**
Tue	5	12:01 AM (0.5) L
Wed	6	12:57 AM (0.4) L
Thu	7 ○	1:51 AM (0.3) L
Fri	8	2:45 AM (0.3) L
Sat	9	3:40 AM (0.3) L
Sun	10	4:35 AM (0.3) L
Mon	11	5:33 AM (0.3) L
Tue	12	6:32 AM (0.4) L
Wed	13	12:17 AM (1.6) **H**
Thu	14	1:12 AM (1.5) **H**
Fri	15	2:10 AM (1.4) **H**
Sat	16	3:07 AM (1.4) **H**
Sun	17	4:01 AM (1.4) **H**
Mon	18	4:51 AM (1.4) **H**
Tue	19	5:37 AM (1.4) **H**
Wed	20	12:33 AM (0.7) L
Thu	21	1:15 AM (0.6) L
Fri	22	1:57 AM (0.5) L
Sat	23 ●	2:40 AM (0.5) L
Sun	24	3:24 AM (0.4) L
Mon	25	4:10 AM (0.4) L
Tue	26	4:58 AM (0.4) L
Wed	27	5:49 AM (0.4) L
Thu	28	6:43 AM (0.4) L
Fri	29	12:30 AM (1.7) **H**
Sat	30	1:33 AM (1.6) **H**
Sun	31	2:39 AM (1.6) **H**

During Daylight Savings Time add one hour to the times stated below.

MAY 2020

Tide 2		Tide 3		Tide 4	
9:05 AM	(0.5) L	3:28 PM	(1.2) **H**	8:45 PM	(0.8) L
10:01 AM	(0.4) L	4:24 PM	(1.3) **H**	9:57 PM	(0.7) L
10:53 AM	(0.4) L	5:14 PM	(1.5) **H**	11:02 PM	(0.6) L
11:41 AM	(0.4) L	6:00 PM	(1.6) **H**		
6:11 AM	(1.7) **H**	12:28 PM	(0.4) L	6:45 PM	(1.7) **H**
7:06 AM	(1.7) **H**	1:13 PM	(0.4) L	7:30 PM	(1.8) **H**
8:00 AM	(1.6) **H**	1:57 PM	(0.4) L	8:15 PM	(1.9) **H**
8:54 AM	(1.6) **H**	2:41 PM	(0.5) L	9:01 PM	(1.9) **H**
9:48 AM	(1.5) **H**	3:25 PM	(0.5) L	9:48 PM	(1.8) **H**
10:43 AM	(1.3) **H**	4:11 PM	(0.6) L	10:36 PM	(1.8) **H**
11:42 AM	(1.2) **H**	4:59 PM	(0.7) L	11:25 PM	(1.7) **H**
12:46 PM	(1.2) **H**	5:51 PM	(0.8) L		
7:32 AM	(0.4) L	1:55 PM	(1.1) **H**	6:51 PM	(0.8) L
8:30 AM	(0.5) L	3:04 PM	(1.2) **H**	7:58 PM	(0.9) L
9:21 AM	(0.5) L	4:00 PM	(1.2) **H**	9:07 PM	(0.9) L
10:04 AM	(0.6) L	4:42 PM	(1.3) **H**	10:10 PM	(0.9) L
10:41 AM	(0.6) L	5:17 PM	(1.4) **H**	11:03 PM	(0.8) L
11:14 AM	(0.6) L	5:48 PM	(1.5) **H**	11:49 PM	(0.8) L
11:47 AM	(0.6) L	6:20 PM	(1.6) **H**		
6:21 AM	(1.4) **H**	12:21 PM	(0.6) L	6:52 PM	(1.7) **H**
7:05 AM	(1.4) **H**	12:56 PM	(0.6) L	7:26 PM	(1.7) **H**
7:50 AM	(1.4) **H**	1:31 PM	(0.6) L	8:02 PM	(1.7) **H**
8:35 AM	(1.3) **H**	2:08 PM	(0.6) L	8:38 PM	(1.7) **H**
9:23 AM	(1.3) **H**	2:46 PM	(0.6) L	9:17 PM	(1.7) **H**
10:12 AM	(1.2) **H**	3:26 PM	(0.7) L	9:58 PM	(1.7) **H**
11:05 AM	(1.2) **H**	4:10 PM	(0.7) L	10:43 PM	(1.7) **H**
12:01 PM	(1.2) **H**	5:03 PM	(0.8) L	11:33 PM	(1.7) **H**
1:00 PM	(1.2) **H**	6:05 PM	(0.8) L		
7:37 AM	(0.4) L	2:00 PM	(1.3) **H**	7:16 PM	(0.8) L
8:32 AM	(0.4) L	2:57 PM	(1.4) **H**	8:30 PM	(0.8) L
9:26 AM	(0.4) L	3:52 PM	(1.5) **H**	9:41 PM	(0.7) L

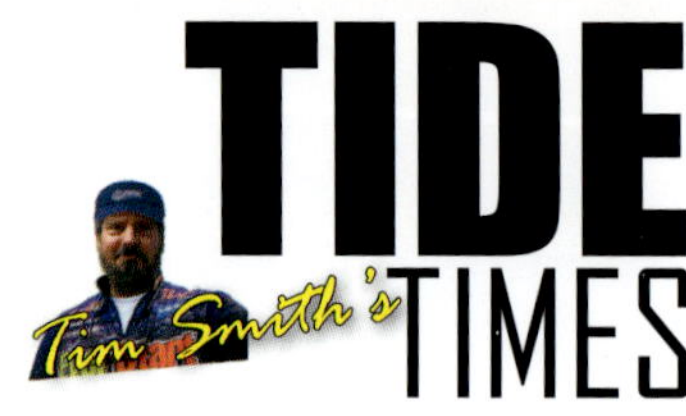

POPULAR TIDE ADJUSTMENTS

Tamboon Inlet	+ 13mins
Mallacoota Inlet	0
Marlo Bar	+ 25min
Sydenham Inlet (Surf Beach)	+ 15min
Point Hicks	+ 7min
Marlo (Snowy River Entrance)	+ 25min

Eden

(Mallacoota)

Day	Date		Tide 1
Mon	1		3:45 AM (1.6) **H**
Tue	2		4:50 AM (1.6) **H**
Wed	3		5:52 AM (1.6) **H**
Thu	4		12:48 AM (0.4) L
Fri	5		1:45 AM (0.3) L
Sat	6	○	2:40 AM (0.3) L
Sun	7		3:33 AM (0.2) L
Mon	8		4:27 AM (0.2) L
Tue	9		5:19 AM (0.3) L
Wed	10		6:10 AM (0.3) L
Thu	11		6:58 AM (0.4) L
Fri	12		12:36 AM (1.5) **H**
Sat	13		1:25 AM (1.4) **H**
Sun	14		2:15 AM (1.4) **H**
Mon	15		3:07 AM (1.3) **H**
Tue	16		4:00 AM (1.3) **H**
Wed	17		4:53 AM (1.3) **H**
Thu	18		12:08 AM (0.7) L
Fri	19		12:53 AM (0.6) L
Sat	20		1:38 AM (0.5) L
Sun	21	●	2:23 AM (0.4) L
Mon	22		3:08 AM (0.3) L
Tue	23		3:53 AM (0.3) L
Wed	24		4:40 AM (0.3) L
Thu	25		5:28 AM (0.3) L
Fri	26		6:17 AM (0.3) L
Sat	27		12:14 AM (1.7) **H**
Sun	28		1:14 AM (1.6) **H**
Mon	29		2:18 AM (1.6) **H**
Tue	30		3:24 AM (1.5) **H**

During Daylight Savings Time add one hour to the times stated below.

JUNE 2020

Tide 2		Tide 3		Tide 4	
10:17 AM	(0.4) L	4:43 PM	(1.6) **H**	10:47 PM	(0.6) L
11:06 AM	(0.4) L	5:32 PM	(1.7) **H**	11:49 PM	(0.5) L
11:54 AM	(0.5) L	6:20 PM	(1.8) **H**		
6:51 AM	(1.5) **H**	12:41 PM	(0.5) L	7:07 PM	(1.9) **H**
7:48 AM	(1.5) **H**	1:27 PM	(0.5) L	7:54 PM	(1.9) **H**
8:44 AM	(1.4) **H**	2:13 PM	(0.5) L	8:41 PM	(1.9) **H**
9:39 AM	(1.3) **H**	2:59 PM	(0.6) L	9:28 PM	(1.8) **H**
10:34 AM	(1.2) **H**	3:46 PM	(0.6) L	10:15 PM	(1.8) **H**
11:29 AM	(1.2) **H**	4:34 PM	(0.7) L	11:02 PM	(1.7) **H**
12:26 PM	(1.2) **H**	5:26 PM	(0.8) L	11:49 PM	(1.6) **H**
1:22 PM	(1.2) **H**	6:22 PM	(0.8) L		
7:44 AM	(0.5) L	2:16 PM	(1.2) **H**	7:24 PM	(0.9) L
8:25 AM	(0.5) L	3:04 PM	(1.3) **H**	8:28 PM	(0.9) L
9:04 AM	(0.6) L	3:47 PM	(1.4) **H**	9:30 PM	(0.9) L
9:41 AM	(0.6) L	4:25 PM	(1.4) **H**	10:28 PM	(0.9) L
10:18 AM	(0.6) L	5:02 PM	(1.5) **H**	11:20 PM	(0.8) L
10:55 AM	(0.6) L	5:38 PM	(1.6) **H**		
5:45 AM	(1.3) **H**	11:34 AM	(0.6) L	6:15 PM	(1.7) **H**
6:37 AM	(1.3) **H**	12:13 PM	(0.6) L	6:52 PM	(1.7) **H**
7:27 AM	(1.2) **H**	12:54 PM	(0.6) L	7:31 PM	(1.7) **H**
8:18 AM	(1.2) **H**	1:35 PM	(0.6) L	8:11 PM	(1.8) **H**
9:07 AM	(1.2) **H**	2:19 PM	(0.6) L	8:54 PM	(1.8) **H**
9:58 AM	(1.2) **H**	3:05 PM	(0.6) L	9:38 PM	(1.8) **H**
10:48 AM	(1.2) **H**	3:56 PM	(0.7) L	10:26 PM	(1.8) **H**
11:40 AM	(1.2) **H**	4:52 PM	(0.7) L	11:18 PM	(1.7) **H**
12:33 PM	(1.3) **H**	5:54 PM	(0.7) L		
7:08 AM	(0.3) L	1:28 PM	(1.4) **H**	7:02 PM	(0.7) L
7:59 AM	(0.4) L	2:23 PM	(1.5) **H**	8:13 PM	(0.7) L
8:52 AM	(0.4) L	3:19 PM	(1.6) **H**	9:25 PM	(0.6) L
9:44 AM	(0.5) L	4:13 PM	(1.7) **H**	10:35 PM	(0.6) L

POPULAR TIDE ADJUSTMENTS

Tamboon Inlet	+ 13mins
Mallacoota Inlet	0
Marlo Bar	+ 25min
Sydenham Inlet (Surf Beach)	+ 15min
Point Hicks	+ 7min
Marlo (Snowy River Entrance)	+ 25min

Eden

(Mallacoota)

Day	Date		Tide 1
Wed	1		4:32 AM (1.5) **H**
Thu	2		5:38 AM (1.4) **H**
Fri	3		12:42 AM (0.4) L
Sat	4		1:39 AM (0.3) L
Sun	5	○	2:32 AM (0.2) L
Mon	6		3:22 AM (0.2) L
Tue	7		4:09 AM (0.2) L
Wed	8		4:53 AM (0.3) L
Thu	9		5:35 AM (0.3) L
Fri	10		6:14 AM (0.4) L
Sat	11		6:51 AM (0.5) L
Sun	12		12:41 AM (1.4) **H**
Mon	13		1:27 AM (1.3) **H**
Tue	14		2:19 AM (1.3) **H**
Wed	15		3:16 AM (1.2) **H**
Thu	16		4:17 AM (1.2) **H**
Fri	17		5:19 AM (1.2) **H**
Sat	18		12:33 AM (0.5) L
Sun	19		1:19 AM (0.4) L
Mon	20		2:03 AM (0.3) L
Tue	21	●	2:46 AM (0.2) L
Wed	22		3:30 AM (0.2) L
Thu	23		4:15 AM (0.2) L
Fri	24		5:00 AM (0.2) L
Sat	25		5:47 AM (0.3) L
Sun	26		6:36 AM (0.3) L
Mon	27		12:56 AM (1.6) **H**
Tue	28		2:00 AM (1.5) **H**
Wed	29		3:10 AM (1.4) **H**
Thu	30		4:23 AM (1.3) **H**
Fri	31		5:34 AM (1.2) **H**

During Daylight Savings Time add one hour to the times stated below.

JULY 2020

Tide 2		Tide 3		Tide 4	
10:35 AM	(0.5) L	5:07 PM	(1.7) **H**	11:41 PM	(0.5) L
11:26 AM	(0.5) L	5:59 PM	(1.8) **H**		
6:41 AM	(1.3) **H**	12:15 PM	(0.5) L	6:49 PM	(1.8) **H**
7:39 AM	(1.3) **H**	1:04 PM	(0.5) L	7:37 PM	(1.8) **H**
8:34 AM	(1.2) **H**	1:51 PM	(0.5) L	8:24 PM	(1.8) **H**
9:25 AM	(1.2) **H**	2:38 PM	(0.6) L	9:09 PM	(1.8) **H**
10:14 AM	(1.2) **H**	3:24 PM	(0.6) L	9:53 PM	(1.7) **H**
11:02 AM	(1.2) **H**	4:11 PM	(0.7) L	10:36 PM	(1.6) **H**
11:48 AM	(1.2) **H**	4:59 PM	(0.7) L	11:17 PM	(1.6) **H**
12:33 PM	(1.2) **H**	5:50 PM	(0.8) L	11:59 PM	(1.5) **H**
1:18 PM	(1.3) **H**	6:46 PM	(0.8) L		
7:28 AM	(0.5) L	2:03 PM	(1.3) **H**	7:45 PM	(0.9) L
8:06 AM	(0.6) L	2:48 PM	(1.4) **H**	8:48 PM	(0.9) L
8:45 AM	(0.6) L	3:32 PM	(1.4) **H**	9:51 PM	(0.8) L
9:26 AM	(0.6) L	4:15 PM	(1.5) **H**	10:50 PM	(0.7) L
10:10 AM	(0.6) L	4:58 PM	(1.5) **H**	11:44 PM	(0.6) L
10:55 AM	(0.6) L	5:40 PM	(1.6) **H**		
6:17 AM	(1.1) **H**	11:41 AM	(0.6) L	6:23 PM	(1.7) **H**
7:11 AM	(1.1) **H**	12:27 PM	(0.6) L	7:06 PM	(1.7) **H**
8:01 AM	(1.2) **H**	1:14 PM	(0.6) L	7:50 PM	(1.8) **H**
8:48 AM	(1.2) **H**	2:02 PM	(0.5) L	8:35 PM	(1.8) **H**
9:35 AM	(1.2) **H**	2:52 PM	(0.5) L	9:22 PM	(1.8) **H**
10:22 AM	(1.3) **H**	3:45 PM	(0.5) L	10:11 PM	(1.8) **H**
11:10 AM	(1.3) **H**	4:41 PM	(0.5) L	11:02 PM	(1.7) **H**
12:00 PM	(1.4) **H**	5:42 PM	(0.6) L	11:57 PM	(1.7) **H**
12:53 PM	(1.5) **H**	6:47 PM	(0.6) L		
7:26 AM	(0.4) L	1:49 PM	(1.5) **H**	7:58 PM	(0.6) L
8:19 AM	(0.5) L	2:47 PM	(1.6) **H**	9:13 PM	(0.5) L
9:14 AM	(0.5) L	3:47 PM	(1.6) **H**	10:27 PM	(0.5) L
10:10 AM	(0.5) L	4:46 PM	(1.7) **H**	11:35 PM	(0.4) L
11:05 AM	(0.5) L	5:42 PM	(1.7) **H**		

POPULAR TIDE ADJUSTMENTS

Tamboon Inlet	+ 13mins
Mallacoota Inlet	0
Marlo Bar	+ 25min
Sydenham Inlet (Surf Beach)	+ 15min
Point Hicks	+ 7min
Marlo (Snowy River Entrance)	+ 25min

Eden

(Mallacoota)

Day	Date		Tide 1	
Sat	1		12:36 AM	(0.3) L
Sun	2		1:30 AM	(0.3) L
Mon	3		2:17 AM	(0.2) L
Tue	4	○	2:59 AM	(0.2) L
Wed	5		3:38 AM	(0.2) L
Thu	6		4:15 AM	(0.3) L
Fri	7		4:49 AM	(0.3) L
Sat	8		5:23 AM	(0.4) L
Sun	9		5:57 AM	(0.5) L
Mon	10		12:03 AM	(1.3) **H**
Tue	11		12:48 AM	(1.3) **H**
Wed	12		1:42 AM	(1.2) **H**
Thu	13		2:46 AM	(1.1) **H**
Fri	14		3:58 AM	(1.1) **H**
Sat	15		5:06 AM	(1.1) **H**
Sun	16		12:10 AM	(0.4) L
Mon	17		12:54 AM	(0.3) L
Tue	18		1:37 AM	(0.2) L
Wed	19	●	2:19 AM	(0.2) L
Thu	20		3:01 AM	(0.2) L
Fri	21		3:44 AM	(0.2) L
Sat	22		4:28 AM	(0.2) L
Sun	23		5:13 AM	(0.3) L
Mon	24		6:01 AM	(0.4) L
Tue	25		12:42 AM	(1.4) **H**
Wed	26		1:49 AM	(1.3) **H**
Thu	27		3:06 AM	(1.2) **H**
Fri	28		4:25 AM	(1.1) **H**
Sat	29		5:35 AM	(1.1) **H**
Sun	30		12:24 AM	(0.3) L
Mon	31		1:10 AM	(0.3) L

During Daylight Savings Time add one hour to the times stated below.

AUGUST 2020

Tide 2		Tide 3		Tide 4	
6:36 AM	(1.2) **H**	11:58 AM	(0.5) L	6:33 PM	(1.7) **H**
7:31 AM	(1.2) **H**	12:48 PM	(0.5) L	7:21 PM	(1.7) **H**
8:19 AM	(1.2) **H**	1:35 PM	(0.5) L	8:06 PM	(1.7) **H**
9:02 AM	(1.2) **H**	2:20 PM	(0.5) L	8:48 PM	(1.7) **H**
9:43 AM	(1.2) **H**	3:04 PM	(0.5) L	9:28 PM	(1.6) **H**
10:21 AM	(1.2) **H**	3:47 PM	(0.6) L	10:06 PM	(1.6) **H**
11:00 AM	(1.3) **H**	4:32 PM	(0.6) L	10:44 PM	(1.5) **H**
11:39 AM	(1.3) **H**	5:18 PM	(0.7) L	11:22 PM	(1.4) **H**
12:19 PM	(1.3) **H**	6:09 PM	(0.7) L		
6:32 AM	(0.5) L	1:02 PM	(1.3) **H**	7:05 PM	(0.8) L
7:10 AM	(0.6) L	1:48 PM	(1.4) **H**	8:08 PM	(0.8) L
7:53 AM	(0.6) L	2:38 PM	(1.4) **H**	9:17 PM	(0.7) L
8:41 AM	(0.7) L	3:29 PM	(1.4) **H**	10:23 PM	(0.7) L
9:33 AM	(0.7) L	4:20 PM	(1.5) **H**	11:20 PM	(0.6) L
10:27 AM	(0.6) L	5:09 PM	(1.5) **H**		
6:04 AM	(1.1) **H**	11:20 AM	(0.6) L	5:57 PM	(1.6) **H**
6:54 AM	(1.1) **H**	12:11 PM	(0.5) L	6:44 PM	(1.7) **H**
7:39 AM	(1.2) **H**	1:01 PM	(0.5) L	7:31 PM	(1.7) **H**
8:23 AM	(1.3) **H**	1:51 PM	(0.4) L	8:18 PM	(1.8) **H**
9:06 AM	(1.3) **H**	2:42 PM	(0.4) L	9:06 PM	(1.8) **H**
9:51 AM	(1.4) **H**	3:34 PM	(0.4) L	9:55 PM	(1.8) **H**
10:37 AM	(1.5) **H**	4:29 PM	(0.4) L	10:47 PM	(1.7) **H**
11:26 AM	(1.5) **H**	5:29 PM	(0.4) L	11:42 PM	(1.6) **H**
12:18 PM	(1.5) **H**	6:34 PM	(0.4) L		
6:53 AM	(0.5) L	1:16 PM	(1.5) **H**	7:46 PM	(0.5) L
7:49 AM	(0.5) L	2:18 PM	(1.5) **H**	9:04 PM	(0.5) L
8:49 AM	(0.6) L	3:23 PM	(1.6) **H**	10:21 PM	(0.4) L
9:52 AM	(0.6) L	4:28 PM	(1.6) **H**	11:28 PM	(0.3) L
10:52 AM	(0.6) L	5:26 PM	(1.6) **H**		
6:30 AM	(1.1) **H**	11:47 AM	(0.6) L	6:17 PM	(1.6) **H**
7:16 AM	(1.2) **H**	12:36 PM	(0.5) L	7:03 PM	(1.6) **H**

POPULAR TIDE ADJUSTMENTS

Location	Adjustment
Tamboon Inlet	+ 13mins
Mallacoota Inlet	0
Marlo Bar	+ 25min
Sydenham Inlet (Surf Beach)	+ 15min
Point Hicks	+ 7min
Marlo (Snowy River Entrance)	+ 25min

Eden

(Mallacoota)

Day	Date	Tide 1
Tue	1	1:50 AM (0.2) L
Wed	2 ○	2:25 AM (0.3) L
Thu	3	2:57 AM (0.3) L
Fri	4	3:28 AM (0.3) L
Sat	5	3:58 AM (0.4) L
Sun	6	4:30 AM (0.4) L
Mon	7	5:03 AM (0.5) L
Tue	8	5:38 AM (0.6) L
Wed	9	12:20 AM (1.2) **H**
Thu	10	1:19 AM (1.1) **H**
Fri	11	2:33 AM (1.0) **H**
Sat	12	3:52 AM (1.0) **H**
Sun	13	4:58 AM (1.1) **H**
Mon	14	5:49 AM (1.1) **H**
Tue	15	12:24 AM (0.3) L
Wed	16	1:06 AM (0.2) L
Thu	17 ●	1:47 AM (0.2) L
Fri	18	2:28 AM (0.2) L
Sat	19	3:10 AM (0.2) L
Sun	20	3:54 AM (0.3) L
Mon	21	4:39 AM (0.3) L
Tue	22	5:27 AM (0.4) L
Wed	23	12:32 AM (1.3) **H**
Thu	24	1:46 AM (1.2) **H**
Fri	25	3:09 AM (1.1) **H**
Sat	26	4:29 AM (1.1) **H**
Sun	27	5:30 AM (1.1) **H**
Mon	28	12:00 AM (0.3) L
Tue	29	12:38 AM (0.3) L
Wed	30	1:11 AM (0.3) L

During Daylight Savings Time add one hour to the times stated below.

SEPTEMBER 2020

Tide 2		Tide 3		Tide 4	
7:54 AM	(1.2) **H**	1:20 PM	(0.5) L	7:44 PM	(1.6) **H**
8:29 AM	(1.2) **H**	2:02 PM	(0.5) L	8:22 PM	(1.6) **H**
9:03 AM	(1.3) **H**	2:43 PM	(0.5) L	8:59 PM	(1.6) **H**
9:37 AM	(1.3) **H**	3:23 PM	(0.5) L	9:35 PM	(1.5) **H**
10:11 AM	(1.4) **H**	4:05 PM	(0.5) L	10:11 PM	(1.4) **H**
10:47 AM	(1.4) **H**	4:49 PM	(0.6) L	10:49 PM	(1.4) **H**
11:25 AM	(1.4) **H**	5:37 PM	(0.6) L	11:31 PM	(1.3) **H**
12:06 PM	(1.4) **H**	6:32 PM	(0.6) L		
6:17 AM	(0.6) L	12:52 PM	(1.4) **H**	7:35 PM	(0.7) L
7:03 AM	(0.7) L	1:45 PM	(1.4) **H**	8:46 PM	(0.6) L
8:00 AM	(0.7) L	2:43 PM	(1.4) **H**	9:54 PM	(0.6) L
9:04 AM	(0.7) L	3:43 PM	(1.4) **H**	10:52 PM	(0.5) L
10:08 AM	(0.7) L	4:40 PM	(1.5) **H**	11:41 PM	(0.4) L
11:06 AM	(0.6) L	5:33 PM	(1.6) **H**		
6:32 AM	(1.2) **H**	11:59 AM	(0.5) L	6:23 PM	(1.7) **H**
7:13 AM	(1.3) **H**	12:50 PM	(0.4) L	7:12 PM	(1.7) **H**
7:54 AM	(1.4) **H**	1:41 PM	(0.3) L	8:00 PM	(1.8) **H**
8:36 AM	(1.5) **H**	2:31 PM	(0.3) L	8:49 PM	(1.7) **H**
9:20 AM	(1.6) **H**	3:24 PM	(0.3) L	9:40 PM	(1.7) **H**
10:05 AM	(1.6) **H**	4:19 PM	(0.3) L	10:32 PM	(1.6) **H**
10:54 AM	(1.6) **H**	5:18 PM	(0.3) L	11:29 PM	(1.4) **H**
11:47 AM	(1.6) **H**	6:24 PM	(0.3) L		
6:20 AM	(0.5) L	12:45 PM	(1.5) **H**	7:37 PM	(0.4) L
7:21 AM	(0.6) L	1:50 PM	(1.5) **H**	8:56 PM	(0.4) L
8:29 AM	(0.7) L	3:00 PM	(1.5) **H**	10:10 PM	(0.4) L
9:39 AM	(0.7) L	4:07 PM	(1.5) **H**	11:11 PM	(0.3) L
10:43 AM	(0.6) L	5:06 PM	(1.5) **H**		
6:15 AM	(1.2) **H**	11:37 AM	(0.6) L	5:56 PM	(1.5) **H**
6:51 AM	(1.2) **H**	12:23 PM	(0.5) L	6:38 PM	(1.5) **H**
7:22 AM	(1.3) **H**	1:04 PM	(0.5) L	7:16 PM	(1.5) **H**

POPULAR TIDE ADJUSTMENTS

Tamboon Inlet	+ 13mins
Mallacoota Inlet	0
Marlo Bar	+ 25min
Sydenham Inlet (Surf Beach)	+ 15min
Point Hicks	+ 7min
Marlo (Snowy River Entrance)	+ 25min

Eden

(Mallacoota)

Day	Date	Tide 1
Thu	1	1:41 AM (0.3) L
Fri	2 ○	2:09 AM (0.4) L
Sat	3	2:38 AM (0.4) L
Sun	4	3:09 AM (0.4) L
Mon	5	3:40 AM (0.5) L
Tue	6	4:13 AM (0.5) L
Wed	7	4:48 AM (0.6) L
Thu	8	12:02 AM (1.1) **H**
Fri	9	1:09 AM (1.0) **H**
Sat	10	2:27 AM (1.0) **H**
Sun	11	3:41 AM (1.0) **H**
Mon	12	4:38 AM (1.1) **H**
Tue	13	5:24 AM (1.2) **H**
Wed	14	6:05 AM (1.4) **H**
Thu	15	12:32 AM (0.2) L
Fri	16	1:13 AM (0.2) L
Sat	17 ●	1:55 AM (0.2) L
Sun	18	2:38 AM (0.3) L
Mon	19	3:22 AM (0.3) L
Tue	20	4:07 AM (0.4) L
Wed	21	4:56 AM (0.5) L
Thu	22	12:26 AM (1.2) **H**
Fri	23	1:43 AM (1.1) **H**
Sat	24	3:07 AM (1.1) **H**
Sun	25	4:19 AM (1.1) **H**
Mon	26	5:10 AM (1.2) **H**
Tue	27	5:47 AM (1.3) **H**
Wed	28	6:18 AM (1.3) **H**
Thu	29	12:24 AM (0.4) L
Fri	30	12:53 AM (0.4) L
Sat	31	1:22 AM (0.4) L

During Daylight Savings Time add one hour to the times stated below.

OCTOBER 2020

Tide 2		Tide 3		Tide 4	
7:52 AM	(1.4) **H**	1:43 PM	(0.5) L	7:52 PM	(1.5) **H**
8:23 AM	(1.4) **H**	2:22 PM	(0.5) L	8:28 PM	(1.5) **H**
8:54 AM	(1.5) **H**	3:01 PM	(0.5) L	9:04 PM	(1.4) **H**
9:27 AM	(1.5) **H**	3:42 PM	(0.5) L	9:42 PM	(1.4) **H**
10:02 AM	(1.5) **H**	4:25 PM	(0.5) L	10:23 PM	(1.3) **H**
10:39 AM	(1.5) **H**	5:13 PM	(0.5) L	11:08 PM	(1.2) **H**
11:19 AM	(1.4) **H**	6:07 PM	(0.5) L		
5:27 AM	(0.7) L	12:04 PM	(1.4) **H**	7:09 PM	(0.5) L
6:18 AM	(0.7) L	12:58 PM	(1.4) **H**	8:16 PM	(0.5) L
7:25 AM	(0.8) L	2:01 PM	(1.4) **H**	9:21 PM	(0.5) L
8:41 AM	(0.8) L	3:07 PM	(1.4) **H**	10:17 PM	(0.4) L
9:51 AM	(0.7) L	4:10 PM	(1.5) **H**	11:06 PM	(0.3) L
10:52 AM	(0.6) L	5:08 PM	(1.6) **H**	11:50 PM	(0.3) L
11:48 AM	(0.5) L	6:02 PM	(1.6) **H**		
6:45 AM	(1.5) **H**	12:40 PM	(0.4) L	6:53 PM	(1.7) **H**
7:26 AM	(1.6) **H**	1:31 PM	(0.3) L	7:44 PM	(1.7) **H**
8:09 AM	(1.7) **H**	2:22 PM	(0.2) L	8:34 PM	(1.6) **H**
8:53 AM	(1.7) **H**	3:15 PM	(0.2) L	9:26 PM	(1.5) **H**
9:39 AM	(1.7) **H**	4:11 PM	(0.2) L	10:21 PM	(1.4) **H**
10:28 AM	(1.7) **H**	5:11 PM	(0.2) L	11:20 PM	(1.3) **H**
11:20 AM	(1.6) **H**	6:16 PM	(0.3) L		
5:50 AM	(0.6) L	12:18 PM	(1.6) **H**	7:26 PM	(0.3) L
6:54 AM	(0.7) L	1:22 PM	(1.5) **H**	8:39 PM	(0.3) L
8:08 AM	(0.7) L	2:30 PM	(1.4) **H**	9:46 PM	(0.4) L
9:23 AM	(0.7) L	3:37 PM	(1.4) **H**	10:39 PM	(0.4) L
10:28 AM	(0.7) L	4:36 PM	(1.4) **H**	11:21 PM	(0.4) L
11:21 AM	(0.7) L	5:24 PM	(1.4) **H**	11:55 PM	(0.4) L
12:05 PM	(0.6) L	6:06 PM	(1.4) **H**		
6:46 AM	(1.4) **H**	12:45 PM	(0.6) L	6:44 PM	(1.4) **H**
7:15 AM	(1.5) **H**	1:23 PM	(0.5) L	7:20 PM	(1.4) **H**
7:45 AM	(1.6) **H**	2:02 PM	(0.5) L	7:58 PM	(1.4) **H**

POPULAR TIDE ADJUSTMENTS

Location	Adjustment
Tamboon Inlet	+ 13mins
Mallacoota Inlet	0
Marlo Bar	+ 25min
Sydenham Inlet (Surf Beach)	+ 15min
Point Hicks	+ 7min
Marlo (Snowy River Entrance)	+ 25min

Eden

(Mallacoota)

Day	Date	Tide 1
Sun	1 ○	1:52 AM (0.4) L
Mon	2	2:24 AM (0.5) L
Tue	3	2:57 AM (0.5) L
Wed	4	3:32 AM (0.6) L
Thu	5	4:08 AM (0.6) L
Fri	6	4:51 AM (0.7) L
Sat	7	12:57 AM (1.0) **H**
Sun	8	2:07 AM (1.1) **H**
Mon	9	3:12 AM (1.1) **H**
Tue	10	4:05 AM (1.2) **H**
Wed	11	4:51 AM (1.4) **H**
Thu	12	5:35 AM (1.5) **H**
Fri	13	6:18 AM (1.6) **H**
Sat	14	12:42 AM (0.3) L
Sun	15 ●	1:25 AM (0.3) L
Mon	16	2:09 AM (0.4) L
Tue	17	2:54 AM (0.4) L
Wed	18	3:41 AM (0.5) L
Thu	19	4:30 AM (0.6) L
Fri	20	12:17 AM (1.1) **H**
Sat	21	1:28 AM (1.1) **H**
Sun	22	2:41 AM (1.1) **H**
Mon	23	3:44 AM (1.2) **H**
Tue	24	4:31 AM (1.2) **H**
Wed	25	5:07 AM (1.3) **H**
Thu	26	5:38 AM (1.4) **H**
Fri	27	6:08 AM (1.5) **H**
Sat	28	12:05 AM (0.5) L
Sun	29	12:38 AM (0.5) L
Mon	30 ○	1:13 AM (0.5) L

During Daylight Savings Time add one hour to the times stated below.

NOVEMBER 2020

Tide 2		Tide 3		Tide 4	
8:17 AM	(1.6) **H**	2:42 PM	(0.4) L	8:37 PM	(1.3) **H**
8:51 AM	(1.6) **H**	3:23 PM	(0.4) L	9:19 PM	(1.3) **H**
9:26 AM	(1.6) **H**	4:07 PM	(0.4) L	10:04 PM	(1.2) **H**
10:03 AM	(1.6) **H**	4:55 PM	(0.4) L	10:54 PM	(1.1) **H**
10:43 AM	(1.5) **H**	5:47 PM	(0.4) L	11:51 PM	(1.1) **H**
11:29 AM	(1.5) **H**	6:44 PM	(0.4) L		
5:46 AM	(0.8) L	12:23 PM	(1.5) **H**	7:44 PM	(0.4) L
6:59 AM	(0.8) L	1:26 PM	(1.5) **H**	8:43 PM	(0.4) L
8:18 AM	(0.8) L	2:34 PM	(1.5) **H**	9:38 PM	(0.4) L
9:31 AM	(0.7) L	3:40 PM	(1.5) **H**	10:27 PM	(0.4) L
10:36 AM	(0.6) L	4:42 PM	(1.6) **H**	11:13 PM	(0.3) L
11:34 AM	(0.5) L	5:40 PM	(1.6) **H**	11:58 PM	(0.3) L
12:29 PM	(0.4) L	6:35 PM	(1.6) **H**		
7:02 AM	(1.8) **H**	1:23 PM	(0.3) L	7:29 PM	(1.6) **H**
7:46 AM	(1.8) **H**	2:16 PM	(0.2) L	8:22 PM	(1.5) **H**
8:32 AM	(1.9) **H**	3:10 PM	(0.1) L	9:17 PM	(1.4) **H**
9:19 AM	(1.8) **H**	4:06 PM	(0.1) L	10:13 PM	(1.3) **H**
10:08 AM	(1.8) **H**	5:04 PM	(0.2) L	11:12 PM	(1.2) **H**
10:59 AM	(1.7) **H**	6:04 PM	(0.2) L		
5:25 AM	(0.7) L	11:53 AM	(1.6) **H**	7:06 PM	(0.3) L
6:27 AM	(0.7) L	12:51 PM	(1.5) **H**	8:08 PM	(0.4) L
7:39 AM	(0.8) L	1:52 PM	(1.4) **H**	9:04 PM	(0.4) L
8:53 AM	(0.8) L	2:53 PM	(1.4) **H**	9:51 PM	(0.5) L
10:00 AM	(0.8) L	3:50 PM	(1.3) **H**	10:29 PM	(0.5) L
10:56 AM	(0.7) L	4:41 PM	(1.3) **H**	11:03 PM	(0.5) L
11:42 AM	(0.7) L	5:26 PM	(1.3) **H**	11:34 PM	(0.5) L
12:24 PM	(0.6) L	6:09 PM	(1.3) **H**		
6:39 AM	(1.6) **H**	1:04 PM	(0.5) L	6:51 PM	(1.3) **H**
7:12 AM	(1.6) **H**	1:45 PM	(0.5) L	7:34 PM	(1.3) **H**
7:46 AM	(1.7) **H**	2:26 PM	(0.4) L	8:17 PM	(1.2) H

POPULAR TIDE ADJUSTMENTS

Tamboon Inlet	+ 13mins
Mallacoota Inlet	0
Marlo Bar	+ 25min
Sydenham Inlet (Surf Beach)	+ 15min
Point Hicks	+ 7min
Marlo (Snowy River Entrance)	+ 25min

Eden

(Mallacoota)

Day	Date	Tide 1
Tue	1	1:48 AM (0.5) L
Wed	2	2:25 AM (0.5) L
Thu	3	3:03 AM (0.6) L
Fri	4	3:44 AM (0.6) L
Sat	5	4:32 AM (0.7) L
Sun	6	12:33 AM (1.1) **H**
Mon	7	1:32 AM (1.2) **H**
Tue	8	2:29 AM (1.2) **H**
Wed	9	3:24 AM (1.4) **H**
Thu	10	4:16 AM (1.5) **H**
Fri	11	5:05 AM (1.6) **H**
Sat	12	5:53 AM (1.7) **H**
Sun	13	12:14 AM (0.4) L
Mon	14	1:01 AM (0.4) L
Tue	15 ●	1:47 AM (0.4) L
Wed	16	2:34 AM (0.4) L
Thu	17	3:22 AM (0.5) L
Fri	18	4:11 AM (0.6) L
Sat	19	5:02 AM (0.6) L
Sun	20	12:53 AM (1.1) **H**
Mon	21	1:50 AM (1.2) **H**
Tue	22	2:44 AM (1.2) **H**
Wed	23	3:32 AM (1.3) **H**
Thu	24	4:14 AM (1.4) **H**
Fri	25	4:52 AM (1.4) **H**
Sat	26	5:29 AM (1.5) **H**
Sun	27	6:05 AM (1.6) **H**
Mon	28	12:01 AM (0.6) L
Tue	29	12:41 AM (0.5) L
Wed	30 ○	1:22 AM (0.5) L
Thu	31	2:03 AM (0.5) L

During Daylight Savings Time add one hour to the times stated below.

DECEMBER 2020

Tide 2		Tide 3		Tide 4	
8:22 AM	(1.7) **H**	3:08 PM	(0.3) L	9:03 PM	(1.2) **H**
8:58 AM	(1.7) **H**	3:52 PM	(0.3) L	9:51 PM	(1.1) **H**
9:37 AM	(1.7) **H**	4:38 PM	(0.3) L	10:42 PM	(1.1) **H**
10:19 AM	(1.6) **H**	5:26 PM	(0.3) L	11:36 PM	(1.1) **H**
11:06 AM	(1.6) **H**	6:17 PM	(0.3) L		
5:30 AM	(0.7) L	11:59 AM	(1.6) **H**	7:10 PM	(0.3) L
6:39 AM	(0.8) L	12:59 PM	(1.5) **H**	8:03 PM	(0.4) L
7:54 AM	(0.7) L	2:04 PM	(1.5) **H**	8:56 PM	(0.4) L
9:09 AM	(0.7) L	3:11 PM	(1.5) **H**	9:48 PM	(0.4) L
10:18 AM	(0.6) L	4:18 PM	(1.5) **H**	10:38 PM	(0.4) L
11:22 AM	(0.5) L	5:22 PM	(1.5) **H**	11:26 PM	(0.4) L
12:21 PM	(0.4) L	6:22 PM	(1.4) **H**		
6:41 AM	(1.8) **H**	1:18 PM	(0.2) L	7:19 PM	(1.4) **H**
7:29 AM	(1.9) **H**	2:13 PM	(0.2) L	8:15 PM	(1.3) **H**
8:16 AM	(1.9) **H**	3:06 PM	(0.1) L	9:10 PM	(1.3) **H**
9:04 AM	(1.8) **H**	3:59 PM	(0.1) L	10:04 PM	(1.2) **H**
9:52 AM	(1.8) **H**	4:52 PM	(0.1) L	10:59 PM	(1.2) **H**
10:39 AM	(1.7) **H**	5:43 PM	(0.2) L	11:55 PM	(1.1) **H**
11:28 AM	(1.6) **H**	6:34 PM	(0.3) L		
5:59 AM	(0.7) L	12:16 PM	(1.5) **H**	7:22 PM	(0.4) L
7:01 AM	(0.8) L	1:06 PM	(1.4) **H**	8:07 PM	(0.5) L
8:08 AM	(0.8) L	1:58 PM	(1.3) **H**	8:48 PM	(0.5) L
9:17 AM	(0.8) L	2:52 PM	(1.3) **H**	9:27 PM	(0.6) L
10:20 AM	(0.8) L	3:48 PM	(1.2) **H**	10:04 PM	(0.6) L
11:14 AM	(0.7) L	4:43 PM	(1.2) **H**	10:42 PM	(0.6) L
12:03 PM	(0.7) L	5:36 PM	(1.2) **H**	11:21 PM	(0.6) L
12:47 PM	(0.6) L	6:27 PM	(1.2) **H**		
6:42 AM	(1.6) **H**	1:29 PM	(0.5) L	7:16 PM	(1.2) **H**
7:20 AM	(1.7) **H**	2:11 PM	(0.4) L	8:04 PM	(1.1) **H**
7:58 AM	(1.7) **H**	2:53 PM	(0.3) L	8:50 PM	(1.1) **H**
8:38 AM	(1.7) **H**	3:35 PM	(0.2) L	9:37 PM	(1.1) H

POPULAR

RIGS

Saltwater Rigs

Surface Float Rig

An excellent surface salmon rig consists of a styrene float, a couple of 4/0 hooks and a small sinker for weight. The hooks are tied on a metre or so of 15 kg monofilament trace and are spaced to hold a full pilchard comfortably. Slip a running ball sinker down the trace right on to the top hook. Then slip on a running styrene float and attach the top of the trace to a good quality swivel. This will allow the float to suspend your bait at the correct depth for feeding salmon. Should you require the bait to be set deeper, simply extend the trace length.

This rig casts reasonably well from a threadline or sidecast outfit and can be modified easily to suit small or large salmon, tommy ruff, tailor (with the inclusion of a light wire trace) and trevally.

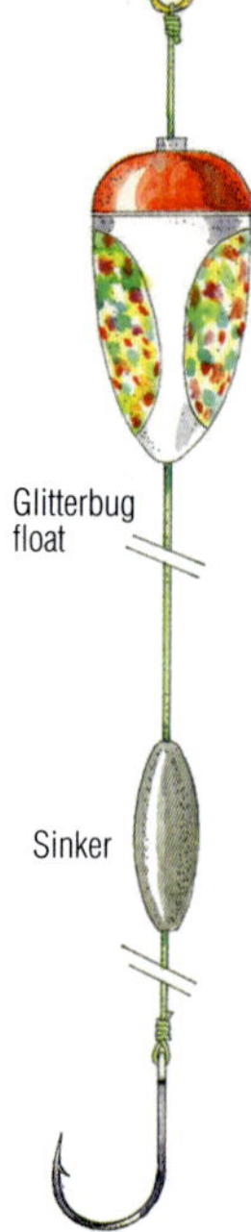

3–6 kg fluorocarbon leader to bait

5 kg mono

Fixed teardrop sinker

Freshwater Rig

Standard Paternoster for Boat and Bank

This is a standard rig for many Australian native species from barra to cod, using anything from a worm, to a yabby, to a live bait or prawn for barra.

You can vary the length of the droppers, depending on conditions, and the 3-way swivel could be substituted with a brass ring if the fish encountered are likely to pull your arms off! Add a red bead too—it can add a touch of spark and get those fish biting.

POPULAR KNOTS

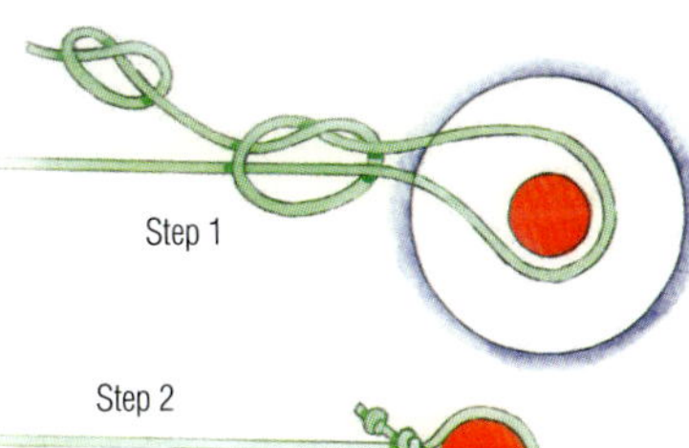

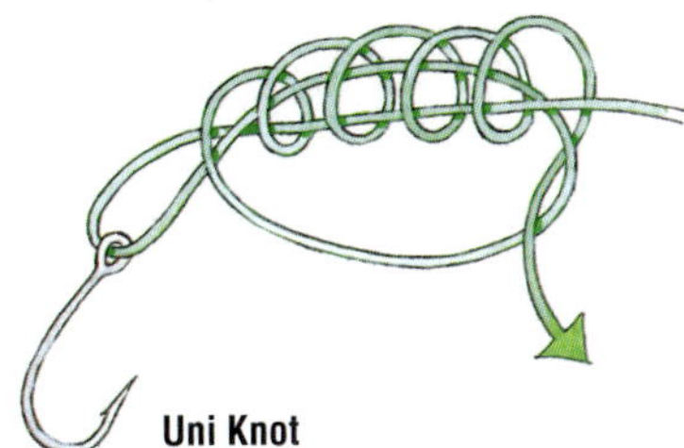

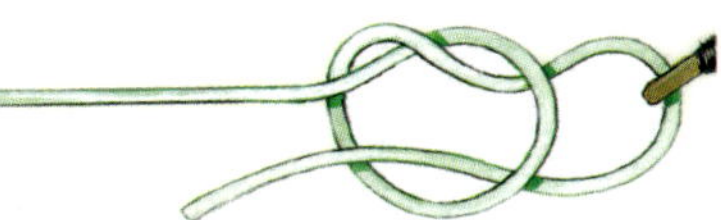

Arbor Knot

This is a very fast and secure knot for attaching line to the reel. Pass the tag end of the line around the spool and form an overhand knot with the tag end around the main line. Then another overhand knot on the tag end of the line. Lubricate the knots if using monofilament, tighten down by pulling the main line, and trim the tag.

Uni Knot

An easy-to-tie versatile knot. Thread the eye of the hook with the line so the hook is suspended on a loop. Encircle the main line with the tag so another loop is formed. Wrap the double strand inside the loop with the tag. Make four wraps in all, leaving the tag protruding from the loop. Close the knot but do not pull it tight just yet. Slide the knot down onto the eye of the hook, pull it tight and trim the tag.

Homer Rhode Knot

This knot should never be used on lighter weight monofilaments, as it breaks at around 50 per cent of the line test.

1. Form an overhand knot in the main line leaving approximately 20 cm (8 inches) of monofilament between the knot and the tag end. Pass the tag end through the hook eye and then back through the overhand knot from the same side as it exited. Tighten the overhand knot lightly to the hook eye by pulling on the tail of the hook and on the tag end of the line, while keeping the two lines parallel to prevent the hook from twisting on the knot.

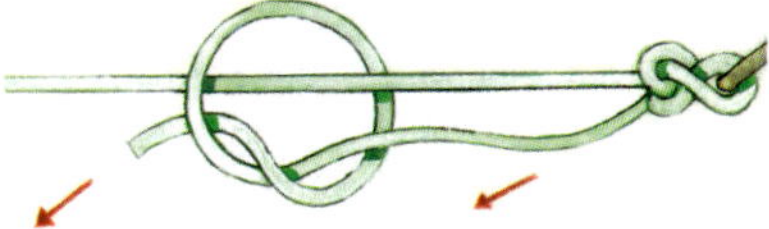

2. Make another overhand knot over the standing part of the line. This knot is the stopper for the loop, so its position determines the size of the loop, generally this knot would be 2–3 cm (1 inch) from the hook eye. Tighten this second knot and then pull on the bend of the hook and the main line at the same time.

3. The knot at the hook eye should slide up the line snugly into the second knot. Trim the tag.

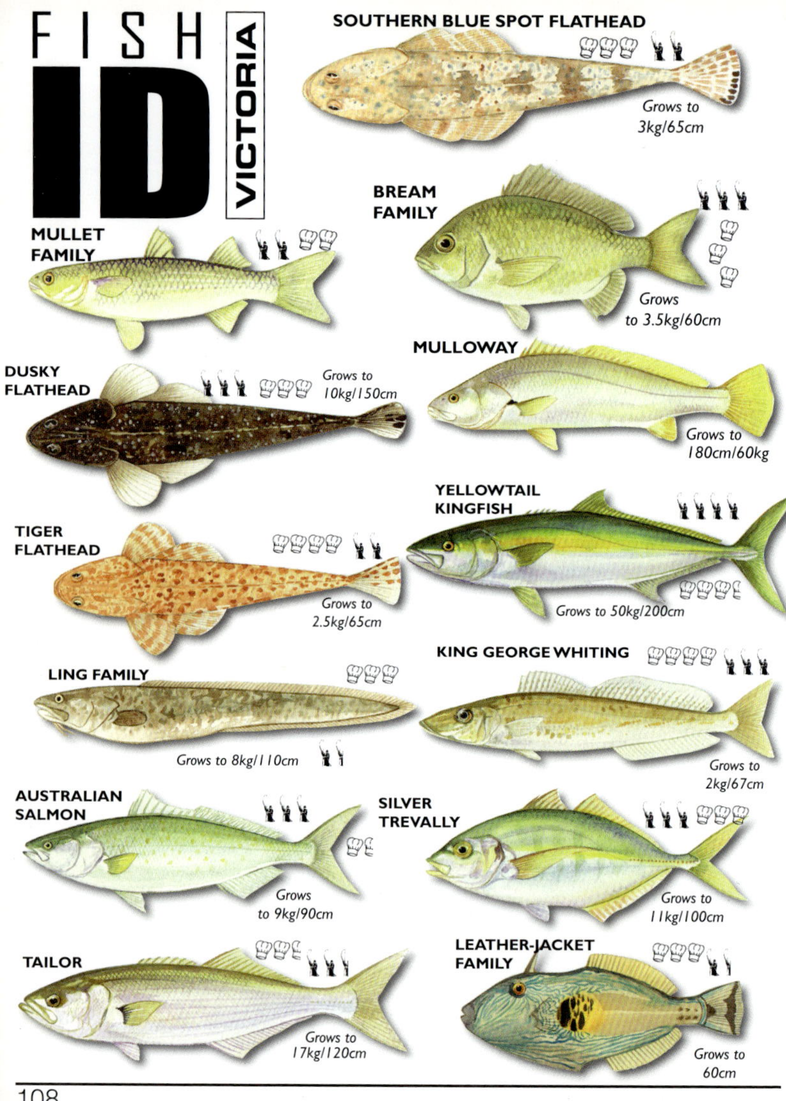

FISH
ID
VICTORIA
SOUTHERN BLUE SPOT FLATHEAD
Grows to 3kg/65cm
BREAM FAMILY
Grows to 3.5kg/60cm
MULLET FAMILY
DUSKY FLATHEAD
Grows to 10kg/150cm
MULLOWAY
Grows to 180cm/60kg
YELLOWTAIL KINGFISH
Grows to 50kg/200cm
TIGER FLATHEAD
Grows to 2.5kg/65cm
KING GEORGE WHITING
Grows to 2kg/67cm
LING FAMILY
Grows to 8kg/110cm
AUSTRALIAN SALMON
Grows to 9kg/90cm
SILVER TREVALLY
Grows to 11kg/100cm
TAILOR
Grows to 17kg/120cm
LEATHER-JACKET FAMILY
Grows to 60cm

BLUETHROAT WRASSE
WRASSE FAMILY
Grows to 40cm/1kg
BARRACOUTA
Grows to 5kg/130cm
FLOUNDER FAMILY
Grows to 1kg/50cm
SNAPPER
Grows to 125cm/19kg
ESTUARY PERCH
Grows to 65cm/7.5kg
MURRAY COD
Grows to 113kg/180cm
REDFIN
Grows to 50cm/3kg
EUROPEAN CARP
Grows to 12kg/100cm
SILVER PERCH
Grows to 60cm/8kg
GOLDEN PERCH
Grows to 70cm/15kg
RAINBOW TROUT
Grows to 80cm/7kg
BROWN TROUT
Grows to 100cm/14kg
AUSTRALIAN BASS
Grows to 4kg/65cm

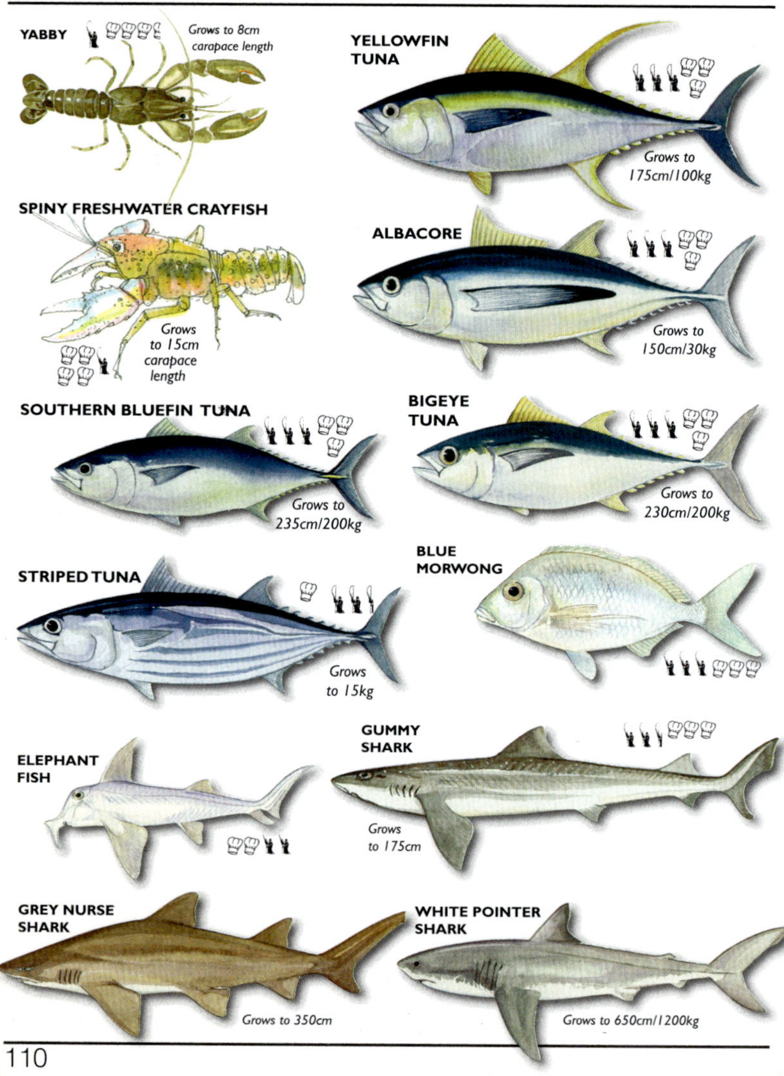
YABBY
Grows to 8cm carapace length
YELLOWFIN TUNA
Grows to 175cm/100kg
SPINY FRESHWATER CRAYFISH
Grows to 15cm carapace length
ALBACORE
Grows to 150cm/30kg
SOUTHERN BLUEFIN TUNA
Grows to 235cm/200kg
BIGEYE TUNA
Grows to 230cm/200kg
STRIPED TUNA
Grows to 15kg
BLUE MORWONG
ELEPHANT FISH
GUMMY SHARK
Grows to 175cm
GREY NURSE SHARK
Grows to 350cm
WHITE POINTER SHARK
Grows to 650cm/1200kg

SQUID

MUSSELS

PRAWNS

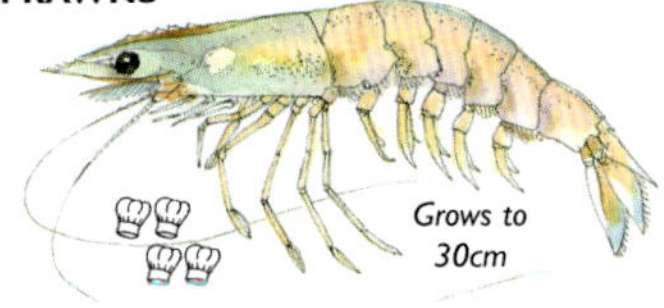

Grows to 30cm

BLUE SPRAT

Grows to 23cm

AUSTRALIAN ANCHOVY

Grows to 23cm

PILCHARD

Grows to 23cm

DANGEROUS AND POISONOUS FISH

TOADFISH

Toxic flesh- never consume

Grows to 15cm

PORCUPINE FISH

Spines deliver painful wounds. Consumption of these fish can result in death.

Grows to 43cm

PUFFER FISH

Toxic flesh: never consume

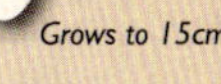

Grows to 15cm

RED GURNARD

Poisonous spines and gill spikes inflict severe pain

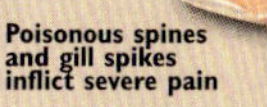

RAY FAMILY

Many rays carry tail bearing spikes that cause injury

Grows to 350cm wide

LEGEND

Poor Sport Fish

Excellent Sport Fish

Poor Eating

Excellent Eating

Potentially dangerous

Not to be consumed